STRAINS OF DISCORD:

Studies in Literary Openness

STRAINS OF DISCORD:
Studies in Literary Openness

~~~~~~~~~~~~~~~~~~~~~~~~~~~~~~~~~~

By ROBERT M. ADAMS

WITH A NEW PREFACE
TO THIS EDITION

Essay Index Reprint Series

BOOKS FOR LIBRARIES PRESS
FREEPORT, NEW YORK

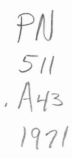
Copyright © 1958 by Cornell University

Reprinted 1971 by arrangement with
Cornell University Press

INTERNATIONAL STANDARD BOOK NUMBER:
0-8369-1917-3

LIBRARY OF CONGRESS CATALOG CARD NUMBER:
75-142601

PRINTED IN THE UNITED STATES OF AMERICA

Si, ne consultant qu'une juste défiance de ses forces, l'auteur eût entouré ses observations de l'appareil inattaquable de ces formes dubitatives et élégantes, qui conviennent si bien à tout homme qui a le malheur de ne pas admirer tout ce qu'admirent les gens en possession de l'opinion publique, sans doute alors les intérêts de sa modestie eussent été parfaitement à couvert; mais il eût parlé bien plus longtemps, et, par le temps qui court, il faut se presser, surtout lorsqu'il s'agit de bagatelles littéraires.

STENDHAL, *Racine et Shakespeare*

PREFACE TO
BOOKS FOR LIBRARIES EDITION

At the time when this book was undergoing a fairly turbulent gestation, some years ago, its title was simply "The Open Form". It carried that name, not only in my mind but on its title page, right into the office of its genial and persuasive publisher. He liked the book all right, but not the title; so, at his request, I changed the latter — not without a certain sense of strain that, I'm afraid, got reflected in the new version. In fact, the change was made against my better judgment; and I think the expanding use, over recent years, of the concept and term "open form" confirms that it really was a better judgment. So, though it's too late to change the title, now that the book has earned itself a small second lease on life, I'd like to memorialize here its original name — the name I still find it possible to repeat without embarrassment.

Robert M. Adams
(Tokyo, Japan, November, 1970)

Preface

THE composition of this book, which has proceeded at an irregular pace over the last five years, was completed for the third and penultimate time while the author held a *Hudson Review* fellowship in literary criticism. For this grant, unsolicited, bounteous, and miraculously opportune, I hasten to express my total gratitude. Generous financial assistance has also come from the Cornell Council on Faculty Research.

The following sections have previously appeared in periodical form: *"Trompe-l'oeil* in Shakespeare and Keats" in the *Sewanee Review;* the first section of "Metaphysical Poets, Ancient and Modern" in the *Kenyon Review;* and the third section of the same chapter in the *Hudson Review.* I am grateful to the editors for permission to reprint. In adapting these essays to the requirements of a volume, I have felt free to modify and on occasion to reverse entirely positions taken in what seems to me now too perfect innocence.

In quoting from *Oedipus Rex* I have used the Penguin version of *The Theban Plays,* translated by E. F. Watling; for Ibsen, the translation by R. F. Sharp in Modern Library's *11 Plays of Henrik Ibsen;* for Shakespeare, the New Cam-

bridge Edition by W. A. Neilson and C. J. Hill (Houghton
Mifflin, 1942); for Keats, the *Complete Poems and Selected
Letters*, edited by C. D. Thorpe (Odyssey Press, 1935);
for Cervantes, the Penguin version translated by J. M.
Cohen; for Flaubert, the translation of *Madame Bovary*
by Eleanor Marx Aveling as it appeared in the old Modern
Library; for Stendhal, C. K. Scott Moncrieff's translation
of *The Red and the Black* (Modern Library); for Eliot,
Collected Poems 1909–1935 (Harcourt, Brace, 1936); for
George Herbert, the *Works*, edited by F. E. Hutchinson
(Oxford, 1941); for Auden, *The Shield of Achilles* (Ran-
dom House, Inc., copyright 1955); for Crashaw, the *Poems*,
edited by L. C. Martin (Oxford, 1927); for Dylan Thomas,
The Collected Poems (New Directions, 1957); for Swift,
A Tale of a Tub (Columbia University Press, 1930); and
for Kafka, *The Penal Colony*, translated by E. and W. Muir
(Schocken Books, 1948). I am grateful to Random House,
Harcourt, Brace, and New Directions for permission to re-
print from works of Auden, Eliot, and Thomas respectively.

A further word of explanation for the language in which
this book is written. It is as plain, literal, specific, and compressed as I could make it. The simplicity of this style may
be misleading. For instance, the fact that I often use the
terminology of mechanism to describe literary works may
suggest that I am exclusively committed to a mechanical
explanation of literary effects. This is wrong. The metaphor
is a convenient and familiar one; and as I am urging a more
liberal interpretation of their own doctrine on the mecha-
nists, it is appropriate to use a metaphor which makes sense
to them. Besides, the metaphor is a good one, as it is flexible
and unpretentious. Using it in this spirit, I have hoped to
find it a vehicle more accessible than any of those special

technical vocabularies with which much modern criticism is marching down the road toward perfectly tight, self-contained, uncommunicating systems. Every literary circumstance worthy a student's interest is doubtless unique. But, being concerned with generalizations, not particulars, I tried to write as plainly as possible, thinking that a simple, literal mind had better work within its own capacity and that, when the regular English vocabulary has been exhausted, there will be plenty of time and many anxious hands to invent new ones.

For the rest, I have built without blueprint or stock pile, picking up what intellectual materials were needed wherever they lay to hand and omitting the cupola and orangery simply because there were no materials to make either. Where possible, I have borrowed freely, and without very systematic acknowledgments, from those who preceded me in particular fields; and I have differed without disputation where I thought myself entitled and obliged to do so. My only excuse for taking such liberties with scholarly method is that the methods of exact demonstration seemed inappropriate to a largely speculative structure. It was not an ultimate architecture at which I aimed, but a temporary, provisional enclosure, serving limited purposes and dedicated to the service of critics.

Robert M. Adams

Ithaca, New York
June 1958

Contents

∽ I ∾

Introduction

EVEN at the risk of getting tangled in the philosopher's web, it may be worth while to begin a book on literary form by defining the subject or trying to define it. No doubt we shall depart from the definition later on, squeezing, distorting, and stretching it to cover unlikely objects for dubious purposes; but definition, though it is not the end of one's ideas, nor even a limit to them, seems safe and useful as a starting point. Let us therefore define.

Form in physical objects is nothing other than a ratio of magnitudes referred to direction in space; it is a quality related to, and perhaps derived from, quantity, or as various medieval schoolmen describe it, *qualitas circa quantitatem,* a phrase which puts the whole thing about as concisely as one could want. Literary works always have form in this sense, though in differing degrees, depending on whether one views them as collections of black marks on white paper or of consecutive noise-symbols. Nor is their physical form always a contemptible element in determining their character. The physical dimensions of a sonnet are matters of some importance; the various ways of dividing its four-teen lines have something to do with the effect it produces, and this effect is relatively distinctive. For instance, mak-

ing the last line an alexandrine would alter the impact of
a sonnet considerably.

Stanzaic forms generally seem susceptible to physical description in significant terms; *rhyme royal* is qualitatively
as well as quantitatively different from *ottava rima*. But
the fact that epics are bound to be long influences somewhat less radically the ways in which they deal with human
nature; and the fact that we have no name for certain forms
of fiction other than "short story" is rather evidence of
an impoverished critical vocabulary than proof that physical dimensions properly characterize a work. For form is
a quality about a quantity, and in literature it seems hard
to define many significant particular qualities in terms of
quantity mechanically conceived. From a full quantitative
description of a sonnet's physical characteristics, its rhythmic patterns and structural divisions, one might, indeed,
get a fairly good idea of its quality, so that, for example,
one might distinguish a sonnet by Milton from a sonnet by
Shakespeare; yet I do not think we should feel that an individual literary form had been fully or even adequately described until something had been said about the pattern of
its assertions.

Here we get, somehow, beyond form as physical phenomenon. It is hard to give numerical value to an assertion.
Yet it is clear that there are commonplace observations and
observations with impact; there are emphatic and unem-
phatic ways of phrasing "the same thing"—if we suppose,
momentarily, that the degree of emphasis is not of the
essence of the thing asserted. And these differences are
quite unrelated to physical dimensions. Physically the magnitude of a sentence may be much the same whether it is
imperative, declarative, or interrogative; yet in a literary

work this distinction would make all the difference in the world. And other examples will easily come to mind of literary qualities which, though immediately distinguished by eye, ear, or mind, cannot be related to a magnitude referred to direction in space.

That physical form is not an exclusive or even a primary ingredient of literary form we learn, among other things, when we see it obtrude in a new way or to a new degree. For instance, we are struck by a peculiarly intrusive quality about shaped verses; they have physical dimension in a more overt sense than we are used to seeing. Even when they aim to represent the absolute peace which surpasses human speech (Herbert's "Altar"), these devices leave us with a sense of curious, intrusive rigor, of a difficulty sought out where none need be, of form unnecessarily overlaid on form. But the point clearly needs no more emphasis. Literary structure is not entirely or essentially physical; it is to a considerable extent a structure of meanings, emphases, and intents, hence better described under the analogy of energy than under that of magnitude.

A structure of tempered and proportioned assertions is not necessarily a structure of literal assertions; in fact, its being a structure almost guarantees that some of its assertions will be determined by structural needs rather than by their relation to a reality outside the poem. But the literary work is uncommitted, one way or the other, with regard to the "truth" of its assertions, measured by an exterior standard. They may be literally true and literally meant; figuratively, typically, or dramatically true; or outrageously and patently untrue. They may contain several different and perhaps contradictory assertions at once—may even be, in an exterior sense, what we call total nonsense.

I mean, not that there is no penalty (i.e., limitation of effects) attached to any of these options, but that there is no reason to judge any of them categorically illegitimate. And this circumstance, while it limits the extent to which literary assertions can be measured against a quantitative standard of veracity, frees us to measure their energies and estimate their tendencies relative to one another.

Thus, to use a simple but dramatic example, the first sonnet of Sidney's *Astrophel and Stella* [1] is built around a contrast between the indirect and direct approaches to its subject which takes full advantage of the stringy, dragged-out effect of English hexameters. The first thirteen lines represent a mock-serious ambition, lofty, lengthy, and multistaged, subject to a series of increasingly rigid frustrations, against which the poet reacts with increasing violence. His program is presented in the roundabout, abstract, and not very logical logic of the first four lines: love leading to verse, verse to pleasure, pleasure to reading, reading to knowledge, knowledge to pity, and pity perhaps to grace. (The verbal figure is that which Putten-

---

[1] "Loving in truth, and fain in verse my love to show,
   That she, dear she, might take some pleasure of my pain,
   Pleasure might cause her read, reading might make her know,
   Knowledge might pity win, and pity grace obtain,
   I sought fit words to paint the blackest face of woe:
   Studying inventions fine, her wits to entertain,
   Oft turning others' leaves, to see if thence would flow
   Some fresh and fruitful showers upon my sunburnt brain.
   But words came halting forth, wanting Invention's stay;
   Invention, Nature's child, fled stepdame Study's blows;
   And others' feet still seemed but strangers in my way.
   Thus, great with child to speak, and helpless in my throes,
   Biting my truant pen, beating myself for spite:
   'Fool,' said my Muse to me, 'look in thy heart, and write!' "

ham calls the climax, or marching figure.) But after this program has been sketched out, the fifth line introduces as a first stage the theme of "seeking fit words"; and the way in which the poet seeks them is expounded in the next six lines. There is comic self-criticism in his description of the search; in fact he has been exposing his quest, even as he expounded it, throughout the poem, but it becomes wholly absurd as he seeks in the dry leaves of others for showers to fall on his sunburnt brain. The "sunburnt brain" provides a comic climax for this self-critical tendency because it is a brain parched by the fires of love, hence barren, but also crazed and incapable of functioning properly—so that the whole search is made to seem mad and unnatural. Thus another sequence of logical abstractions comes to be arrayed against it; Nature and her child Invention are brought into close and violent contrast with stepdame Study, the whole culminating in a line of relatively quiet, but complete, rejection of the search for "fit words" in the writings of others—and so, by implication, of the total program (line 11).

But for the last three lines the metaphors become still more violent as they revert to, reverse, and complicate previous images; instead of being a barren field which needs only water, the poet's mind is now a pregnant woman, frantic with pain but helpless—till the Muse, stepping in to free her child from the blows and bindings of stepdame Study, leaves the grammar of lines 12 and 13 in total suspense and delivers her final peremptory, contemptuous admonition. Her speech not only exemplifies what it recommends by sounding natural; it sets the whole elaborate program and anguished impasse of the first thirteen lines against "real" Nature, urging that it is an artificial dilemma and an unnecessary one. Thus the sequence of "forces" in the poem might be summarized this way: a playful program of literary love-making is expounded, ridiculously frustrated, then raised in intensity and horror to a point where it is collapsed and resolved by the admonitions of the Muse.

The precise details of this exemplary analysis are less important than its general character; analyses of this sort are perfectly commonplace today, and I have indulged this one at length only because it implies, and makes clear that it implies, a certain concept of literary structure or form. Literary form as I think most people conceive of it nowadays is the geometry of assertions, their structure, their interrelations, their patternings. It is not so much *qualitas circa quantitatem* as *qualitas intra vires*, a quality growing out of a complex of related energies. What I describe metaphorically as energy is really emphasis or impact, and the critical task often resolves itself into measuring its quantity and direction.

Many equally commonplace arguments suggest that the quality of the structure, rather than the quality of its component energies, contributes most to the literary effect. Everyone is familiar with the untutored poet who pours vast energy into his verse and produces only feeble mawk because he has no sense of patterning and structuring his language. A turgid, emphatic style strikes us as ridiculous today, its emphases are not adequately tempered or structured. Literature, again, often describes atrociously disagreeable and distasteful events—from which the reader, nevertheless, derives profound satisfaction. That satisfaction is certainly not due to fine language or to any sort of prettification, but to the organizing of the reader's responses by means of structured literary forms, i.e., patterns of assertion. One of the great and seminal principles of modern criticism is, precisely, formalism; with the conceivable exception of the archetypalists, almost every major critical school of our day has been centrally concerned with the problem of literary form. The only apparent reason for this widespread preoccupation is that literary form is very important in relation to the isue of literary merit itself.

The meanings of which literary form is composed have undergone various interesting descriptions, from I. A. Richards' account of them as "pseudo-statements," through Suzanne Langer's notion of them as "virtual" or presumptive assertions, to Northrop Frye's fiery yet cloudy declaration that they comprise a complete autonomous body of knowledge, a total structure. Our present purposes inviting us to emphasize the structure in preference to the components, it may be useful to turn rather arbitrarily to a single figure, Kenneth Burke, whose way of describing the typical action of literature is through analogy with four other structured and directed yet impractical, or at least removed and indirectly manipulative, activities: the dream, the chart, the game, and the charm or prayer. All these forms of activity, along with the plastic and musical arts, and especially literature, are, in Burke's terms, modes of symbolic action.

It is good to have the matter stated in these terms, because symbolic action implies a resolution or working out of the situation with which the literary work purports to deal. Games are usually mock fights, and they are not much fun unless somebody wins, hence the institution of "keeping score." Dreams used to and may still be described as serving to protect sleep, hence the concept of dream work, a psychic displacement and distortion of what might otherwise be too clearly perceived. Prayers and charts imply a focusing and definition of purpose which need not be severely practical but are usually indirectly so. The terminology of pseudo-statements or virtual statements implies that the pleasure of art can be the pleasure of unstructured fantasy; it lays a heavy emphasis on the notion of "as if," which becomes the implicit syntax of every artistic assertion. As for Frye's cosmic unity, it denies, at least to the mundane mind of this reader, the pleasure of accepting the work of art as a thing-in-itself, with the different marks of its differences fresh upon it. But Burke's formulation gives the reader as well as the writer an active role in literature; it invites him to control as well as to participate in the activity; to be flexible and yielding and various as well as insistent in his relation to the "meanings" of art. The reader reads literature to get a medicine, a magic; to train himself, as it were, in the difficult disciplines of experience; to act out symbolically triumphs which may strengthen him, or failures which may protect him, against the hostile energies of life itself. He aims to shape himself in a desired attitude which may (and not simply magically) evoke from the outside world a desired response.

It is a charming and a useful way of approaching literature, rich in pedagogic possibilities, fascinating in its appeal to subtle and aggressive minds like that of Burke. Few critical theories incite one to such imaginative and inventive reading; few leave one freer to participate in the literary work yet bind one so distinctly to observe the rules of the actual game he is playing. Yet the metaphor of symbolic action, like most such metaphors, implies a number of notions about literary form which would not be endorsed immediately, unanimously, and without question if they were put forward as separate propositions. It implies that literary works typically constitute self-contained constellations of forces, yet they are often deliberately impure in this respect. What shall we do, as formalist critics, about that great half-relevant lecture on the art of war which occurs in the course of Tolstoi's *War and Peace?* Moreover, some literary works are unfinished. What can we say, on formalist assumptions, about Balzac's "Comédie humaine," which never achieved the completeness even of an outline? Finally, some literary works purposely derogate the aesthetic effect. What sort of formal critical judgment can we reach regarding *The Good Woman of Setzuan,* by Brecht, who deliberately declined to resolve its field of forces?

None of these examples represents a central figure in modern critical theory (perhaps this says something about modern critical theory). But it is not hard to find an example, right from the heart of "the tradition," of a poem which raises the question of unresolved and indeterminate literary form without, perhaps, answering it. T. S. Eliot has in the past betrayed some doubt as to the precise character of Donne's wit. Should one describe it as a vast jumble of incoherent erudition through which Donne meanders, carrying on a puzzled and humorous shuffling of the pieces and betraying a manifest fissure between thought and sensibility? Or should one, rather, call attention to the remarkable unity of Donne's intellectual and emotional life, his ability to feel his thought as immediately as the odor of a rose? The question of fact is an interesting and difficult one, perhaps too difficult for a categorical answer; but its consequences are just as interesting and even more difficult. Suppose one accepts the first option; is it an impeachment of Donne to think him a divided and fragmentary sensibility? To be sure, he might have learned from Aristotle and other critics that unity in literature is preferable to diversity; but it is clear too that he did not write for Aristotle. When he wrote, he had chiefly in mind to render the fresh, raw experience of everyday life; and the passionate apprehension of particulars which so delights us in his poetry was quite incompatible with the pertinacious pursuit of certain sorts of unity.

But if Donne was not trying to be unified, why should we hold him to this standard, whether he succeeded or failed? His success would have been inadvertent, as his failure was incidental to other aims. No doubt he was reared under lax and deplorable standards. But what cause do we advance by holding him to a criterion of which he never heard, though it was established by Théophile Gautier himself? However correct the judgment pronounced against him, might he not plead invincible ignorance? It is a good plea in more exalted circumstances. I think I know certain critics who would not hesitate to be more just than Justice itself; but it is not yet proved that we advance our literary enjoyment or understanding by applying even admirable standards indiscriminately. They say in France that "le meilleur est l'ennemi du bien." Universal criteria of social behavior are not nearly so popular as they once were; and universal standards of literary excellence seem—perhaps because they make everything so rigid and easy once we have them—like such meritorious things that they had better be approached only gradually and with caution. Just as a point of tactics, one would rather see extreme critical multiplicity gently coaxed toward moderate diversity than absolute uniformity ruthlessly extended as far as possible from a single center.

Donne's "Third Satire" concerns true religion. The poet urges, with great emphasis, that true religion is the most important thing on earth. One must seek it with all his heart and soul. But where is it? The poet does not know. He lists the alternatives under the rather coarse figure of a set of wenches who are attractive to men of various humors; he strongly derogates the idea of accepting any religious position on the basis of someone else's authority; and he concludes without "getting anywhere," by repeating his original injunction to look hard for true religion, wherever it is. In several senses this is a completely unified poem, structurally. It is about one subject, it is spoken by a single "voice," it is all in one tonality, it may even be described as passing the reader in a single cycle from the importance of religion to the need for finding true religion back to the importance of religion. It uses a consistent metrical form, it employs assertions which are gramatically complete, it is consecutive and consequential. Its imagery is various and vigorous in conformity with the subject, which is the strenuous search for truth. On the other hand, one obvious element of unresolvedness or irresolution in the poem bulks very large in its total effect. The poet never decides which is true religion—never decides, in fact, on what basis one can properly decide which is true religion. He recognizes the need for decision:

> but unmoved thou
> Of force must one, and forc'd but one allow;
> And the right.

But he does not take a step in the direction of decision. On the contrary; though the poem is all about the urgency of

deciding, the chief decisions which are reached are in favor
of continued indecision:

> To adore, or scorne an image, or protest,
> May all be bad; doubt wisely; in strange way
> To stand inquiring right, is not to stray;
> To sleepe, or run wrong, is.

Now it is clear that failure to reach a decision may be a
terminal, a unified and unifying conclusion in a literary
work quite as much as decision itself. As the assertions
made in such a work need not be true in an exterior sense,
the resolutions it propounds need not be logically conse-
quent; and in fact, there need not be any "logical" conclusions at all. An emotional conclusion, a change in attitude
and point of view, is just as good as a change in logical
relationships—perhaps better. For literature as a structure
of meanings is less concerned with describing or changing
the relations among things than with describing or changing human attitudes toward things. There is a purity about
leaving things exactly as they are in order to show that
looking at them from a different angle alters their significance entirely. But, this passing point aside, whether a
literary work seems conclusive or not depends on how it is
structured. From one point of view the "Third Satire" is
more strictly unified because its end is, practically, its beginning; from another aspect, this structural quality leaves
the poem unresolved in a major way. The sense of urgency
which fills it is not shown to have an outlet; the arguments
which are strenuously propounded in the middle of the
work only lead back to the situation which gave rise to
them. In this respect the poem is indeterminate or unresolved—not that it fails to solve a certain "practical"

problem which it set itself but rather that it both fails this way and fails to represent its failure as a fresh discovery. But the terminology of "failure" betrays me here. I think we are dealing, not with an unsuccessful effort to resolve the theme, but with a perfectly successful effort to write a poem which should be, in certain respects, unresolved. This is a matter of intent, not personally, but structurally conceived; it represents one variety of what I should like to describe as a literary work in "open form."

The open form is literary form (a structure of meanings, intents, and emphases, i.e., verbal gestures) which includes a major unresolved conflict with the intent of displaying its unresolvedness. Certain varieties of openness are deliberately excluded from this definition, largely for practical reasons. Fragments, for example, are of no particular interest to this study. There is a sense, surely, in which works like "Hyperion," *The Mystery of Edwin Drood*, "Kubla Khan," *The Faerie Queene*, and "The Triumph of Life" are all open in form, for the complexly related structures of words, ideas, and feelings which their authors set out to create were never finished. Fragments, however, do not constitute a recognized literary mode, nor often, for that matter, so much as an interesting accident. Frequently the determining cause of a fragment is merely the most tiresome of outside intrusions, death, distraction, or ennui having broken in to mar a fair or perhaps an overambitious conception. An interesting footnote to literary history might be provided by the attitude which authors and editors have taken toward fragments. Milton's preservation of a single juvenile fragment on "The Passion" is, I suspect, a relative rarity for the age; discounting *juvenilia*, well over a third of the items in Shelley's collected poems are de-

scribed as fragments or canceled passages, and Keats was
not ashamed to publish, as presumably finished work,
"Hyperion," both versions of which break off abruptly in
the middle of the action, in the middle of a sentence, and
in the middle of a line. But from the technical aspect of
literary form there is really very little to say of fragments
except that what form they have is usually hypothetical.

Not much more interesting are those types of literary
activity the authors of which, under the impulsion of one
fad or another, tried to dispense with formal structure altogether. "Automatic writing" had a vogue some years
ago, under pseudo-Freudian and surrealist auspices; and
Louis Aragon achieved an apt poem titled "Suicide," which
disdained to arrange the letters of the alphabet in any
particular order, simply allowing them to assume their
natural sequence, abcdefghijklmnopqrstuvwxyz. This is
abnegating the authorial self and allowing the poem to
write itself, with a vengeance, though it is not very con-
ducive to literary variety. From spectacularly unstructured
poems like this we may range widely through streamy, free-
associated poetry and slice-of-life novels without finding
much more to say about the structure than that it is deliberately minimal. One may be amused to note that primitivism
has led its followers so far in the rejection of that strict
patterning which is the chief feature of primitive art. But
this is a passing irony. We approach our subject rather more
closely when we come to deal with literary works that are
structured in a number of respects but not in some particular one.

Yet the subject still needs narrowing, to eliminate from
consideration the perverse and the accidental. There is no

particular critical interest in tricks or gadgets, where the refusal to resolve is deliberate and flatfooted, as for instance in Frank Stockton's short story "The Lady or the Tiger?" Here the point of the story is to build up concern over an event and then decline to narrate it. There are some interesting aspects to the device as Stockton uses it. It perversely fulfills the requirements of the story by failing to complete it. It challenges the reader's definition of himself and of the situation to which he has entrusted himself. But essentially "The Lady or the Tiger?" is a trick story, told for the sake of the trick. It fractures that tacit covenant on the basis of which a reader trusts himself to an author's hands, and fractures it, not to make a point, but simply for fun. Like all good jokes, this one is made for the joke's sake; and as my interest in the open form involves essentially the question what it is good for, it has seemed permissible merely to note the existence of jokes, riddles, puzzles, shaggy-dog stories, and similar exhibitions of openness, which are pursued simply because they disappoint temporarily or permanently an expectation of "closedness," and to exclude them from my main accounting.

On the other hand, it is also clear that few or no literary forms are completely closed on every conceivable level. The dead king must have a successor; the happy marriage will or will not have children. The lover who achieves "grace" is probably only at the beginning of his problems. Death itself is not a finality. Even *Hamlet*, which has killed off eight major characters before the final curtain falls, could be prolonged by anyone perverse enough to care about young Fortinbras' accomplishments as a monarch or Hamlet's fate in the other world. Donne's "Third Satire," which strikes the most casual reader as a notably irresolute poem, is, as we have seen, resolved on something like eight levels out of nine.

Thus the open form seems even at first blush to be a notably open concept. On the left flank it is divided by an indefinite, quantitative line from perverse or general formlessness and indeterminacy; on the right, by an equally indefinite, quantitative line from a form which impresses us as pre-eminently closed, even though it has open elements. Yet it may be useful to treat open and closed forms as qualitatively distinct in order to see, if we can, whether there is some rationale, other than perverseness on the one hand or clumsiness and accident on the other, for a work which deliberately declines to resolve its assertion-patterns in a major way. Motivation may provide a basis for the category, as the category makes possible isolation of the motivations; it is circular logic, but none the worse for that as long as there is room in the circle for the observation of facts, the *petits faits vrais*, on which all literary discussion depends.

It would be particularly gratifying, though it is not necessary, to find an aesthetic rationale for the open form, because works of this character are largely ignored in most aesthetic systems. But I do not believe they are all oddities or accidents, and the problem of judging them cannot be permanently shunted aside. To be sure, conventional aesthetic history has a number of stylistic terms to describe devices associated with the open form: "mannerist," "high baroque," "metaphysical," *précieux*, "rococo," "fantastic," "grotesque," and so on down the line to "meretricious." None of these adjectives quite covers the ground (the historical and critical categories behind them are limited), but their intersecting segments cut off a good deal of it. And in particular contexts—for example, the plays of Tieck, Pirandello, or the later Shakespeare—or in dealing with various devices of surrealist art (conflicting reality-levels, *trompe-l'oeil*, etc.), critics have been obliged to cope, often on a catch-as-catch-can basis, with varieties of open-formed work. But systematic discussion of the facts, let alone the issues, has evaded my notice.

The present book, then, undertakes first of all to observe and classify some varieties of open-formed literary works and to define the effects they produce. A corollary to this undertaking is the consideration of whether special criteria may not be appropriate to the judgment of open-formed works or whether a slight adjustment of already existing criteria, a modest shift of emphasis, will not suffice. Finally, I should like to apply the distinction, so far as I can carry it, to considerations more general, perhaps even more historical, than literary. Does the open form serve to express one sort of world view, one definition of the human situation, better than another? Has it any inherent limitations, either as a literary form, a literary device, or as a critical concept—or, conversely, does it have any special adaptabilities which make it suitable to certain literary objectives and modes? To suggest answers to all these questions is in itself an ambitious undertaking for a preliminary work predestined to modest dimensions. Hence the works of literature cited and sometimes analyzed here are intended to serve simply as examples. They are not fully discussed, as if for their own sakes, nor are any more of them brought into the discussion than will serve to illustrate the points being made. Lists and categories, species, genera, and all the paraphernalia of systematic description must remain topics for another occasion, preferably a remote one. Finally, I must implore the reader that he will suppose my generalizations, even those which seem most dogmatic, to be followed by a string of invisible question marks. Once embarked on a set of eccentric speculations like this, the writer is bound to push forward in order to see what he can make of them as a whole; the niceties come later, if at all. Meanwhile, exact grammatical forms notwithstanding, the assertions which follow are intended as a sequence of interrogatives around a central theme. I should like to begin with a contrast between two well-known works of classical antiquity in which the open and closed forms are exemplified with more than archetypal clarity.

∽ II ∽

Oedipus Rex and
The Bacchae

LITERARY discussions of *Oedipus Rex* often center upon the problem of a tragic flaw in the protagonist. Aristotle undeniably asserts that the tragic hero should be, as well as an eminent man, "a man who is brought low through some error of judgment or shortcoming"; but he never specifies what error Oedipus committed. Much ingenuity has been expended to make good the omission, some arguing that a certain "flaw in the inward eye," a "blindness of impulse" is the failing of Oedipus, others that his fault is his "insistence on knowing the truth," and still others that "his weakness and his strength equally betray him." [1] The last idea seems best, but it raises a nice question about *hamartia;* why should an audience care to see a man punished for being strong or virtuous?

Of course no elaborate argument is needed to establish that Oedipus does display in certain actions of the play an impulsive, a proud, and an authoritarian character. On the

---

[1] Lane Cooper, *Aristotle on the Art of Poetry* (New York, 1913), p. 41; Gilbert Norwood, *Greek Tragedy* (4th ed.; London, 1948), p. 149; H. D. F. Kitto, *Greek Tragedy* (London, 1948), p. 140.

other hand, the notion that this character is responsible for his downfall does not seem to be energetically enforced by the structure of the play. Oedipus is not culpably blind to the future consequences of his acts; he looks as far into the future as any man can reasonably be expected to look. Indeed, his final downfall seems to be due as much to his foresight as to his impulsiveness. If he had not fled from Corinth to avoid the fulfillment of the oracle, he would never have killed Laius or met Jocasta. In sending to the oracle for advice he twice acted prudently and, indeed, reverently; in swearing to fulfill its behest he undoubtedly pronounced doom on himself, but not rashly; as a king he could do nothing else. Doubtless, he is an imperfect character; for instance, his mistrust of Creon and Tiresias seems to border on the morbid. But suspicion is not the cause of his downfall, as lack of suspicion would not have averted it; indeed, there is no reason to suppose that, had he possessed all the multiplied and rarefied virtues of the Admirable Crichton, the fate of Oedipus would have been any the less certain.

The whole question of what constitutes a perfect stage character enters here and complicates the issue. The complicating circumstance is that a character with too many virtues forfeits the sympathy of the audience, not only on the grounds that he is plainly exemplary, but because he is bound to seem self-conscious. On the stage, as in life, perfection is suspicious and unnatural; besides, perfection is in one sense at odds with character. Simply to have a character an actor must assume certain characteristics, and from some point of view every characteristic must seem like a failing. To display the simplest elements of kingship an actor must behave with authority; it is a necessity of the position. Nothing is sharper and truer to circumstance than the last words of Creon as he puts on the robes of Oedipus' fallen authority: "Command no more. Obey. Your rule is ended." The words are spoken in answer to Oedipus' plea that his daughters be allowed to accompany him, and their impact is particularly blunt and brutal because, as the story goes, Ismene and Antigone did remain with their father. Still, Sophocles wanted to show that power in its very nature is abrupt and unfeeling; we may conclude that Oedipus' "impulsive" character was partly a quality of his office, and hence that no special idea of guilt attaches to this behavior since it is not a falling off from any supposed or actual ideal of character. Kings ought to behave as if they had authority because they do.

There is in fact a certain hollowness about the whole discussion as I have paraphrased it, because it presupposes that a tragedy is a species of moral lecture illustrated by examples of moral failings—that its pattern is inversely exemplary and might be summarized, "If you are not more temperate or humble or foresighted than Oedipus, this is what will happen to you." As a matter of moral indoctrination, this is probably a very satisfactory formula; indeed, much of the going moral code is based on this sort of thinking, which is often described as "making an example of someone." But tragedy does not properly have the effect of inculcating moral beliefs, so much as of purging the beholder; it does not fill the viewer with an earnest moral resolve to behave better than the protagonist, but with a sense of religious awe.[2] From this point of view a disparity be-

[2] "The reversal of Oedipus is not then a meaningless calamity, but seen as a demonstration of the validity of divine prescience it runs dangerously close to the opposite extreme: it may be a calamity which has too much meaning to be tragic. Such a demonstration

tween the protagonist's flaw and his fate is not only desirable but necessary. And thus, in the consideration of *Oedipus*, we are entitled to by-pass those hairsplitting discussions of whether the hero was too rash or too lethargic—discussions which cast Apollo or the critic or both in the role of superfastidious, hypercritical moral pedant—in order to concentrate on more significant issues.

For the flaw of Oedipus was his fate, the doom pronounced by the oracle at the time of his birth; it was not a personal failing. The most terrible point of the play is not that the happy destiny of Oedipus was marred by a particular mistake he made but that the normal destiny of every man who has the courage to try to know himself and so to control his fate includes the destiny of Oedipus. And with this consideration we approach the problem of the sphinx and the role of this fable in the story.

The defeat of the sphinx and the answering of the riddle, two elements of the story which in versions earlier than that of Sophocles are clearly separable, both relate intimately to initiatory rites; and there seems no doubt that a deeply felt political moral is implied in the whole Oedipus fable. Oedipus, as Marie Delcourt brilliantly argues, is a conqueror; even his incest has the overtone that by uniting with his mother earth he takes possession of his homeland. The sphinx, as a symbol of royal power, evidently carries

---

seems a subject more apt for tract than tragedy; it seems to call for homily or philosophic discourse as its medium rather than the drama" (Bernard M. W. Knox, *Oedipus at Thebes* [New Haven, 1957], p. 50). This is a brilliant insight regarding the doubly dangerous relation between a tragedy and its "meaning"; yet the total effect of Mr. Knox's own subsequent argument, cleverly identifying Oedipus with Athens as the *tyrannoi* of Thebes and Greece respectively, is to bring the play even closer to a lecture.

out these social overtones; and, on these terms, Oedipus is essentially a prince whose coming to power is marked out according to the pattern: exile, return, initiation, conflict with the old king, victory, marriage, and assumption of authority. This pattern provides one sort of moral center for the story in an image of Oedipus as a conqueror, an overreacher. But the sphinx is also a sexual creature, and the story as Sophocles reproduces it gives special play to the sense of sexual horror. The grotesque Oriental beast woman who eats up the young men of Thebes has many earmarks of a fable more primitive than politics itself, even of a nightmare. Mlle. Delcourt has much to tell us of the sexual proclivities of sphinxes and similar creatures—*"avides de sang et de plaisir erotique,"* imposing on their victims *"trois sortes d'épreuves: leurs caresses, leurs coups, et leurs questions."* She relates them not so much to Oriental symbols of monarchical power as to fantasies of nightmare origin and to religious concepts of dead souls, winged and thirsty for human blood. Thus on two or three levels the sphinx story links a political fable with a sexual one. The conquest of the sphinx is a key to political authority; it implies a brag about the power of the brain to solve problems; it also opens the way to marriage with a princess. To possess one's mother is to possess the earth, one's motherland; it is also to be dead and buried. To conquer the sphinx is a high proof of sexual audacity, another evidence of which is sexual possession of one's mother; the penalty of failure is immediate death.

Hence it is appropriate on several levels that the sphinx should ask a question to which the proper answer is "Man" (many sphinxes ask meaningless or arbitrary riddles, but not this one); for besides the conqueror image another

moral center of the story resides in Oedipus' assumption of
normal masculine sexuality. On these terms the sphinx is
not to be identified with Jocasta herself but is merely the
door through which Oedipus passes to find Jocasta. As he
seeks to possess the earth and finds full possession only in
the grave, so he seeks sexual fulfillment and finds it only in
his mother. Success is the doorway to failure. Against the
bitch goddess who threatens to castrate and devour, he
poses his own awareness of what man is. To do this is to be
a king, and to be a king is unequivocally good; it is to pass
the three tests of manhood—those provided by war, wisdom, and sex. To be a king is every man's proper destiny,
and all men properly reverence the one who has discovered
and accomplished it. The first words of Oedipus, entering
on stage, bear witness to the old, intimate relation through
which he has assumed authority over and responsibility for
them: "Children," he calls them, "new blood of Cadmus'
ancient line." As king, Oedipus is father of his people, and
the people need a father. And yet by assuming the office of
paternity, Oedipus, who is himself still one of the children,
finds himself involved in the black crimes of incest and
parricide.

The fault of Oedipus, then, is the fault of all fathers; all
authority (like all affection) descends by a line of usurpa-
tion; and the peremptory impulse in which some have seen
Oedipus' "tragic flaw" is a necessary condition of his greatness, of his simple existence on a level above contempt.
Hubris for Oedipus is inseparable from what one might
describe as "normal" authority, "normal" sexuality; what
one observes in him is not an eccentric ambition instruc-
tively defeated, not a disease developed to ripeness, but a
perfectly normal line of development cut short by the dis-

covery of an essential contradiction or corruption. The story has a peculiar and devastating impact precisely because Oedipus is a man like all other men at their best. He does not commit any obvious errors, and his fate does not invite us to make moral resolutions about behaving better. The play simply purges an audience of the guilt and fear which they share with Oedipus. Pity enters into the total reaction, no doubt, but not under the aspect of purging. Fear and guilt are both self-regarding emotions; pity, as it is essentially other-regarding, does not require or undergo purging. Pity discharges itself on pitiable objects; that is, it is available to us only in so far as we do not identify with the tragic hero but view him from the outside. This is not by any means an improper reaction, but it is not typically tragic, as are the self-regarding emotions of terror and guilt.

From the aspect of literary form it would be hard to find a play more rigidly unified than *Oedipus Rex*. To be sure, the temporal beginning lies more or less open; the play has, in fact, no strict beginning in time, or, rather, it reaches freely past its own opening scene to refer to time before the outbreak of the plague. On the other hand, this is common literary practice; almost all literary forms allow free reference to precedent time and create no sense of violated form by doing so. Indeed, it is almost assumed of stage plays that the short span of their action will represent the culmination of a lengthy previous development. *Oedipus* is not unified simply in this sense, nor simply in the sense that all the action flows from certain main premises and relations between the characters. This too is true enough; the action of Sophocles' play is beautifully articulated, so that the same messenger who brings good tidings, in trying to cap the climax of his news, plunges Oedipus into even

deeper pits of despair. But in calling *Oedipus Rex* a model
of unified form I mean simply that it effects, through
identification with the protagonist's deep-seated guilt and
fear, a massive purgation of the audience and leaves them in
a state of purified repose and contemplation. The chorus,
in chanting its last words, rounds off our vision of Oedipus
and his change; speaking from the outside, impersonally, it
describes the action of the play and voices the moral, not
in the manner of one giving advice to the audience but as
if to solidify the whole play into a concrete nugget of
moral law and satisfied feeling. In this sense the play is a
self-contained unit; there is nothing within it which calls
attention to or criticizes its aesthetic existence; there is no
unresolved or discordant element to disturb its conclusion;
in its psychological effects it is a unified and harmonious
whole that passes the audience through a clear, easily defined, and complete emotional cycle to a distinct logical
and emotional conclusion.

To say so much of *Oedipus* may seem like saying very
little, for according to many familiar aesthetic theories all
successful works of art aim to be unified and harmonious
wholes. But to modify this misconception we need look no
further than some of the plays of Euripides, which are
formed on such a different pattern and yield such a different effect as to seem products of an entirely different
intention. Hippolytus, for instance, in the play to which
he has given his name, is subject to a distinct delusion; he
tries deliberately to live by the worship of Artemis, in-
terpreting this creed to mean that he must scorn Aphrodite.
The neglected deity punishes him, and the moral could not
be more distinctly inculcated: "You must not make the
gods angry." Even the curious scene in which Artemis

tells Hippolytus, by way of consolation, that she will kill one of Aphrodite's favorite mortals does not really alter this characteristic of the drama. It sets the deities in a strange light; an audience of human beings might well look with some misgivings on the gods' rather liberal attitude toward scapegoats. But, aside from altering somewhat the conditions of the moral (it is harder to please the gods than at first appeared), the scene does not alter the exemplary pattern of the play or make any easier the audience's identification with the hero. Here indeed is the crux of the difference. Conceivably fanatics for hunting and chastity with a faint distaste for the vulgar many and a touch of homosexuality in their backgrounds might identify with Hippolytus, but this is not an effect on which the author could count in the majority of his audience. The errors of Hippolytus are distinctly marked early in the drama, they are clearly exemplary in character, and they are specifically responsible for his downfall. Thus the audience observes, not a religious spectacle, but a carefully worked-out problem in moral mechanics. It departs, not in a state of religious purgation, but with a problem to mull over, a message to meditate.

If this is true of the *Hippolytus,* it is true in an even more emphatic sense of Euripides' curious last play, the fascinating drama of *The Bacchae.* Debates over this drama have multiplied so remarkably over the last fifty years as to render even a perfunctory summary of the scholarship disproportionate to a study of this kind. Books by Verrall, Murray, Grube, Norwood, Kitto, Winnington-Ingram and others have pulverized the issues; but no clear pattern of thought emerges. Most of the debates concern a quarrel between the deity Dionysus and the human figure of

Pentheus; and the question is simply where our sympathies are supposed to lie. Some critics have supposed that Pentheus is intended to have our total sympathy. His is a rational, critical intelligence, quick to note the many absurdities of the Dionysian religion intruding from the East and fearless in exposing them. When he is torn to pieces by his own delirious mother on the slopes of Mount Cithaeron, no other reaction can be anticipated from an audience than that of shock and sympathy for the human victim, outrage and distaste for the brutal divinity who so savagely asserts his power. And if we conceive of Euripides as a wholehearted rationalist, his dislike for the deity of drunkenness and inspiration is surely the main theme of the play. This view can be supported by material from the other plays; the gods of Euripides are prone to act like human beings, and as often as they do so, they are likely to be criticized, either tacitly or overtly.

On the other hand, it seems possible to take substantially the opposite view of the play. Critics with a different outlook have seen it as a play in which the inadequacies of a narrow rationalism, exemplified by Pentheus, are fully exposed. The destruction of Pentheus, on these terms, is a little rough and tactless; but only sentimentality would see it as the object of Euripides' main criticism. When one represses the forces of irrational inspiration, even with the loftiest intentions in the world, when one denies (like Pentheus and Hippolytus) the basic energies of one's own nature, they take a terrible revenge. This is the message of the play; but the point is not that the revenge is terrible or the revenger brutal. Rather the point is that the prudent man had better not provoke gods who may be irrational and are certainly powerful. From this aspect the play may well be read as a partial recantation of certain earlier and more intransigent expressions of Euripides' rationalism. Grudging and partial as it may be, *The Bacchae* contains a tribute to the forces of inspiration and a warning that one may not lightly flaunt them.

By way of escaping the critical controversies one might as well register immediately one's conviction that there is truth in both these views of the play, in spite of the fact that they are logically contradictory. The play itself is contradictory; it is saying two different things at once, and one token of this fact is precisely that scholars, after all these years and volumes, show no signs of reaching agreement. Amassing further evidence and splitting new consequences out of the old materials thus seem like less amusing occupations than exploring the consequences of an admission that agreement is impossible. Suppose the play itself is divided in its message and impact; suppose we find it extravagant to identify wholeheartedly with either Pentheus or Dionysus because the whole point of the play is that man exists in a divided and contradictory position, subject to conflicting demands. What effect do these admissions have on our judgment of the play's form and structure?

In the first place, it is clear that the narrative structure of *The Bacchae* is as single and simple as that of *Oedipus*. Dionysus, acting through the agency of Pentheus' mother, Aglave, overthrows the king of Thebes and asserts his own divinity. The god is first imprisoned, then rises to overthrow his jailer. To be sure, the rise of Dionysus involves necessarily the downfall of Pentheus, as one of two wrestlers cannot gain an advantage without his opponent's suffering a loss. Just so, in *Oedipus*, the hero's loss is Creon's

(not to say, Apollo's) gain. But the action itself of *The
Bacchae* is no less unified than that of *Oedipus;* nor, for
that matter, is its impact on the audience diffused in any
major way. The incompatibility of two moral laws is a
single topic, capable of as precise a definition as any other;
and, though it does not invite quite the sort of identification which the testing of a single law does, the self-
consciousness to which it gives rise may be no less deep,
complex, unified, and various in its effect on the reader.

Categorical inferiority is, then, out of the question; nor
are the consequences of this view extravagant so far as its
effect upon our reading of *The Bacchae* proper is concerned. Considering solely the moral preachments, we have
no reason for demanding that a preacher be "for" or
"against" a figure like Dionysus; the preaching is all the
better if we read it as an assertion of impasse. How else
can one deal in rational discourse with the irrational aspects
of man? And from the aspect of drama we lose little more
than a pathetic identification with Pentheus or an over-
weening one with Dionysus. In exchange for this sense of
psychological nearness, so easily available to the dramatist
who will play tricks for it, we gain a sort of inward tension,
an invitation to self-knowledge, which is rare and wonderful. On any other basis our problem is to salvage something from the play. Pentheus, after all, is an unimpressive
sort of king compared with, say, Oedipus or Agammem-
non; if his downfall from high estate is supposed to be a
central theme of the drama, the most primitive dramatist
would have shown him once or twice in a truly regal
posture. As for Dionysus, reading the play with him at the
center converts it from the genre of tragedy entirely into
a romance in which perils are overcome and a superior

authority vindicates his inherent but disputed superiority. But reading the play with the conflict of two disparate spheres of existence at the center of the story leads one to intellectualize its impact, narrowing and yet making more direct the appeal of its exemplary characters, rendering the sympathy judgments less weighty, the identifications less complete, and the psychological patterning of the reader's reactions altogether different. Instead of relieving, the play's structure intensifies the audience's feelings of malaise and guilt; instead of promoting identification and transfer, the play promotes self-questioning and self-consciousness. Its final psychological effect is a sense of anguish, not a sense of release. The play appeals much less directly than does *Oedipus* to a recognizable pleasure principle because within it the state of bondage is ultimate. On the other hand, *The Bacchae* is faithful to a reality principle in its refusal to admit of religious or semi-religious scapegoating; in an adult community actors do not really relieve anyone's guilt by acting out guilty behavior, and Euripides' actors do not pretend to do so. In its bitter insistence on the indefeasibility of both man's contradictory moral obligations, in the strain which it imposes upon one's self-awareness, *The Bacchae* lays claim to an existence beyond the aesthetic level, seeking to act on the reader's conscience directly and permanently, not by mock magic.

But our discussion need not stop with the recognition, all too obvious to begin with, that *Oedipus Rex* and *The Bacchae* are two different plays. They represent, in fact, two different sorts of literary form. These two varieties of literary form are not only different formally but different in something as ultimate as the psychological patterning and responses of the audience. A first principle lies concealed here which had, perhaps, best be made explicit, even at the cost of abstractness; it is that the psychological effects of a literary experience are often less obscure than their imputed causes and may, consequently, provide a firmer ground for literary categorization. Both plays are traditionally described as "tragedies" for reasons that are in good measure conventional: a "serious" theme, characters of some social dignity, an "unhappy" ending. On the whole, this terminology need not be challenged or restricted; but at least one must concede that *Oedipus Rex* and *The Bacchae* are tragedies of very different sorts. No fearful consequences seem to flow from an admission that Greek tragedy took several different forms; *Prometheus Bound* has long been admitted to have a totally different effect from either of the two plays under discussion. If we take the two plays of Sophocles and Euripides as examples of two different literary forms, such a distinction may be perfectly compatible with the label of "tragedy." The difference is simply that between a work which, by resolving its given problems, leaves the audience in a state of psychological repose, emptied of passion, and one which, by failing or refusing to resolve its given problems, leaves the audience in a state of psychological tension, of unreleased anguish.

A number of possible correlations suggest themselves immediately. Euripides was a radical, a hostile critic of current social mores and current religious beliefs, whose mind was largely given to questioning and skepticism and who tended to "endorse" a rational individualism. Sophocles seems to have been a far more conservative man, less interested in scattered showers of dialectical brilliance, more concerned with the comprehensive, unitary view which underlies a collective aspiration like religion. Against this, we must set the fact that, whatever else it is, *The Bacchae* is not a radical play. Nothing would have been easier than to make it such a play, simply by adding a scene or a chorus in which Pentheus or the chorus vindicated his proceedings or associated the injustice of Dionysus with known cruelties of the Olympians. The play would be more radical if it were less open. But such a "closing" neither occurs nor can be imagined as occurring without a radical loss of literary dimension. The play leaves the viewer alone with his guilt; its effect is to isolate and burden, not to associate and purge. But this distinction does not correspond at all to the division between radical and conservative. It is much closer to the line between an individual and a collective view of experience. These views are themselves by-products of other intellectual impulses and concerns; no man ever set out deliberately to be an individualist or a collectivist. Yet there may be constellations of even secondary literary-intellectual patterns; and the view that man is essentially alone with his responsibilities in a complex and divided cosmos seems to be somehow congenial to an open literary form. A handy example for testing the hypothesis is "the modern Euripides," Henrik Ibsen.

∽ III ∽

Two Plays by Ibsen

LATELY Ibsen has come a little out of the shadows to which the early twentieth century casually consigned the later nineteenth; but popular opinion seems still deeply contaminated by errors about Ibsen against which Joyce was protesting more than half a century ago. These confusions cluster thickest around that "manifesto of feminism," *A Doll's House*, and that "stage-treatise on venereal disease," *Ghosts*. Here error is so deeply incrusted on error as to provide good digging for a Schliemann.

One cannot start discussing *A Doll's House* from a better vantage than Frau Hedvig Neimann-Raabe's blunt refusal to assume the part of Nora in the North-German production on the grounds that she herself would never think of abandoning her children.[1] As an international actress of considerable standing and full experience, Frau Neimann-Raabe must be cleared at once of any suspicion that she naïvely equated life with art. Although her training had been that of an ingénue, she cannot have been ignorant that an actress may play Clytemnestra, Lady Macbeth, or even Medea in the evening and wake up in the morning a reputable lady, responsible for no crimes of blood. One notes

[1] Halvdan Koht, *The Life of Ibsen* (New York, 1931), II, 154.

that she did not decline the part on the grounds that it might have an ill effect on the audience, might lead to the downfall of middle-class families and the desertion of bank managers' children. Her revulsion was not social but personal; the play attacked not a set of beliefs or a code of behavior but herself as a person; and it did so in a way and to a degree which this seasoned performer simply could not endure. She was responding, perhaps oddly, to the peculiar weight and impact of a peculiarly shaped play, the full peculiarity of which can be seen only in relation to its central theme.

A clear clue to the character of that theme is provided by Torvald Helmer early in the third act. Up to this point he has had little or nothing to say to the all-important Mrs. Linde; has scarcely exchanged three words with her; and, in fact, considers her (as he will say a moment later) a frightful bore. But she has come in to admire Nora's party finery and is just leaving, when suddenly, as he sees her out, the sparse and silent Torvald blossoms into speech on a most unlikely topic:

Helmer: Is this yours, this knitting?
Mrs. Linde (taking it): Yes, thank you, I had nearly forgotten it.
Helmer: So you knit?
Mrs. Linde: Of course.
Helmer: Do you know, you ought to embroider.
Mrs. Linde: Really? Why?
Helmer: Yes, it's far more becoming. Let me show you. You hold the embroidery thus in your left hand, and use the needle with the right . . . like this . . . with a long, easy sweep. Do you see?
Mrs. Linde: Yes, perhaps . . .
Helmer: But in the case of knitting . . . that can never be any-

thing but ungraceful; look here . . . the arms close together,
the knitting-needles going up and down . . . it has a sort of
Chinese effect. . . . That was really excellent champagne
they gave us.

To be sure, he is a little high, and the scene emphasizes this
fact. But it also points a moral direction. On the most superficial level it shows Torvald as a meddling, self-important,
insensitive person—and goes far out of its way to do so.
Indeed, the play goes so far out of its way, the point is so
slight in itself and so firmly established by previous action,
that the scene on these terms may appear something of a
sore thumb. Ibsen's art, his glancing, sinuous, allusive, indirect dialogue, was fully adequate to make this point in a
less blunt, conspicuous, and untimely way, and had, in fact,
already done so. But in this scene the dialogue is not intended to show that Torvald sets Christine right in trivial
matters; it serves to reveal his bias (something deeper even
than his character) as incurably aesthetic. On a question
as trivial as that of knitting versus embroidery he is guided
by appearances. He never asks what she is making or recalls her circumstances, still embittered and desperate for
anything he knows to the contrary. He simply judges the
performance by the grace of the performer. The audience
is reminded that he has just pulled his wife off the dance
floor, by main strength and in spite of her protests, because
he wants her to make an effective exit and gain a fine
aesthetic effect.

Indeed, as one looks back on the earlier part of the play,
it is to be seen that Torvald has been concerned throughout
with appearances; his life is one long composition, and he
dislikes his wife's dancing of the tarantella—with what a
sure instinct!—because it "surpasses a little the bounds of

art." Even his objection to Krogstad is not moral but aesthetic; "I might have overlooked his moral failings," he says, but Krogstad persists in violating the picture of Torvald the unapproachable bank manager. The whole Helmer household, in fact, is built on a bit of timely retouching undertaken by Torvald in connection with Nora's father; whitewashing papa's peccadillos was evidently the occasion of his first meeting with her.

Torvald Helmer is such a solid bourgeois lump on the stage that it may require a little imagination to see him as a personification of the artist, the aesthete. Still, Ibsen is known to have had a sly, underhanded sense of humor about these things; and the aesthetic view of life as defined by Kierkegaard covers a great deal more territory than in conventional English, where the overtones of the word limit it to Bunthornes with lilies in their medieval hands. For Ibsen, the exponent of aestheticism almost always had a little of the official in his composition, witness, for example, the Mayor and the Pastor in *Brand*, Parson Manders in *Ghosts*, Parson Strawman in *Love's Comedy*, and so on. He had, after all, a strong conviction, not unlike Flaubert's, that in every notary there lurks the debris of a poet; he was also deeply aware of the nineteenth-century tendency to frock-coat even genuine Apollos, and, perhaps thinking of the mixture of spheres which resulted, he was profoundly moved by the thought of fish afraid of the water, an owl terrified of the dark. He spoke frequently of his own calling as that of a state satirist.

The advantage of seeing Torvald as an aesthete, if one decides to do so, is that it relieves one of the obligation to consider him an unusually bad man. He is not by any means a villain; on the contrary, he is unusually kind and nice.

What he does he does for the best; his preoccupations are those of the other characters and of the play as a whole. The arrangement of surfaces is all he or they care about, and all the audience has been asked to care about. Patching, arranging, concealing, half revealing—this is from the ethical point of view a contemptible way to live, but it is the very stuff of dramatic comedy. The audience has been let in on Nora's big secret as it is let in on her addiction to macaroons, on the tacit premise that the only question it will ask is, Will she get away with it?

Indeed, the game of macaroon hiding is pursued with genuine zest by actors and audience for two and a half acts; as Krogstad's letter gets stuck in the letter box, agonizingly out of everyone's reach, as Nora contemplates romantic gambits for ending the game with everyone dissolved in tears for the beautiful Mrs. Helmer, or as she edges coyly up to Dr. Rank, her escape fantasy, tempting him with those scandalous flesh-colored stockings and then jumping back at the first sign that fantasy may turn into reality. In following this game the audience gives its primary sympathy to Nora, of course, if for no better reason than that she draws a pompous lecture for nibbling on a macaroon, thus acquiring the essential sympathy-position of underdog. But in giving Nora first call on its affections (she is, in all seriousness, the play's most capacious vessel of experience), the audience does not wholly reject Torvald. The game is only a game of macaroons; and, while we play it against him, he remains the father-figure who will bail us out if we should happen to lose. The game is, in fact, penny ante; the host (Ibsen-Torvald) knows we are playing only for diversion; he will ensure that even the loser will not go home more than fifty cents out of pocket. Before we have

ventured very deeply into the play, a fifteen-cent bet has
come to stand in the mind of the audience for a royal flush.
In a word, the symbols are inflated. Ibsen has inflated them,
no less (and not much more) than the usual domestic
comedy inflates them, and involved us in the game so
deeply that we forget completely what (if anything) lies
behind the successful concealment or discovery of that
macaroon in the mailbox.

We forget; we are drawn into the play's tissue of hid-
ings and seekings; we lose with Krogstad's first letter, we
win with his second; but at the last minute it is Torvald
who becomes the player as Nora steps aside; and when he
has counted up his gains and losses, it is she who coldly
picks up the hand, the deck, the game itself, and the table
and throws them all in her husband's (as well as the audience's) blank face. The last half of the last act, from the
moment when Nora sits down across the table from her
husband, is a brilliantly destructive attack on Torvald, on
the life of arrangement and appearance, on the audience
which has connived at and accepted such an order of values.
The point of view from which this attack is launched does
not find, in Nora, a very distinct or positive exponent; though
she knows perfectly well what she does not want and can
talk it to death with the most incisive, spare, strong speech
of which stage people are capable, she cannot very well
say what she does want. Partly, no doubt, this inadequacy
is due to the commitments which have been established for
her in the first part of the play. On the stage, at least, Mi-
nerva cannot spring in full armor from the head of Torvald
Helmer's little squirrel. Even as it is, many readers have
testified that Nora's turnabout seems incredible. Certainly
it is radical; but Ibsen's art limits the change to funda-

mentals. Nora is not illuminated; she merely accepts the consequences of an ignorance which remains unchanged by a declaration of intentions. For what it is worth, she proclaims her intention of looking for a saving truth; but Ibsen did not much care whether one supposed she would find it or not, for he gave her no program more definite than bewilderment itself. The point he wanted to make was not that she had become a better person but that she had become a different one. The play represents a qualitative, not a quantitative change. Nora's ideas and feelings are not much clearer at the end of the play than they were at the beginning. Only her premises have changed; and Christine Linde, who has done so much to change them, provides the play's best positive indication of where the new premises lead.

For Christine is altogether at home in the chilly realm of ethical behavior; in the ladylike contest with Nora which furnishes the framework for so much of Ibsen's early exposition, she makes clear that she knows solitude, bitterness, and the truth about herself, that she is a thoroughly resolved and disappointed character. There is an angry, falling finality to her dialogue with Nora about her first husband.

Nora: Poor thing, how you must have suffered. And he left you nothing?
Mrs. Linde: No.
Nora: And no children?
Mrs. Linde: No.
Nora: Nothing at all, then?
Mrs. Linde: Not even any sorrow or grief to live upon.

Mrs. Linde, then, is the precursor of Nora in the wilderness; and Ibsen undoubtedly intended her arrangement with Krogstad, chilly and businesslike as it is, to set off the romantic falsities of the Helmer ménage. Indeed, the *mariage de convenance* represented for Ibsen a kind of ideal; analogous arrangements, like those of Svanhild with Guldstad in *Love's Comedy*, Old Werle with Mrs. Sorby in *The Wild Duck*, and Bolletta Wangel with Arnholm in *The Lady from the Sea*, all seem to be straightforwardly treated, without any satiric criticism of their blunt, flat, unromantic character. They are unromantic and undramatic—antiromantic and antidramatic, rather; but a limited arrangement conducted with antiseptic honesty is, apparently, all the ethical personality can salvage from the universal shipwreck of human folly and weakness. Not only are the strong hard put to redeem themselves, they are perilous to others. Simple contact with these armed, resolute, and bitter souls carries a danger for domestic types. However one regards the breakdown of the Helmer ménage (from Nora's point of view it can scarcely seem better than a desperate necessary venture), Mrs. Linde is clearly responsible for it; her choice to let in the light of truth on this misguided family leads to Nora's more anguished choice, which can only lead, in its turn, to further and harder choices. Clearly, both ladies are in the grip of that terrible Kierkegaardian dilemma which held even Brand helpless in the tension of a demand for "all-or-nothing"; both are committed, at the play's end, to a strenuous course of which the only dramatized aspect is its unremitting austerity.

As it happens, the motive behind this curiously unpleasant antinomy has never been made clear to the present writer. Nothing could be more evident than the proposition that different stadia of human activity exist; the ac-

quisitive, the ethical, and the religious are perfectly distinct spheres, but why one must choose irrevocably to
operate in a single one to the exclusion of both the others
has never been made evident. Ibsen felt, and undertook
to represent, this necessity; it was almost a first principle
of his thought. But neither he nor Kierkegaard ever suc-
ceded, except by the device of caricaturing vulgar eclecti-
cism, in making clear, either in logic or in drama, why
"all-or-nothing" is required of any man by any sphere of
life.

Still, though he could not make its rational basis clear,
Ibsen had the intuition of "all-or-nothing" as man's lot
on earth and was entitled to use it in artistic work. And
one has not quite faced up to the impact of *A Doll's House*
till one has observed that truth within the play not only
liberates the strong Mrs. Linde but in the same action goes
a long way toward destroying the weak Nora; that an
appetite for truth destroys the play itself as a tissue of
limited conflicts; and that this perception of the destructive power of truth is brought to bear, in the most direct
way conceivable, on the audience as an audience and the
actors as aesthetic performers. No wonder Frau Neimann-
Raabe felt that she must be willing to give up her own children and her own family in the name of truth if she were
to play Nora honestly. Her first intuition was truer than
the compromises with which she later covered it over—
playing the role first with a patched-up "happy ending"
and then, when the play had been fussed over by feather-
headed feminists, in its original form. The effect would
not be so shocking if life as a series of moral demands
merely intruded on the aesthetic preoccupations of the
play from some recognized area outside the stage. The

peculiarity is that within the play a character tears herself loose from that delusion (to which the stage is irrevocably committed) that life is to be lived in terms of effects, arrangements, and appearances and departs for some unknown area, angrily blaming everyone for conspiring to make her a marionette and the theater a doll's house. The charges are true; the audience is the veritable villain of the play.

Perhaps it is hard to conceive of a theater which, while remaining a theater, has ceased to be a doll's house; at the risk of seeming ignobly naïve, I must confess I cannot easily picture such an institution. Perhaps the point is simply that as an *institution* it is inconceivable. In any event, *A Doll's House* does something to remind us of the boundless superficiality of theatrical sympathy-judgments as contrasted with the anguished urgency of a genuine moral sense. Why, after all, has the audience liked Nora? Because she nibbled macaroons and was scolded for it; because she did a technically "wrong" thing for a generous reason; because she was weak and spoiled and confused and helpless—or, if not for these precise reasons, then for reasons which are probably worse rather than better, in any strict moral sense. Ibsen's moral sense was nothing if not strict. After the great éclat of *Brand*, his first success, he spoke slightingly of it, saying that he had hoped to produce a great action but had merely written a play. With *A Doll's House* he fulfilled what seems to have been a major ambition, to write a play which was also a moral action; the impact of the work is the impact of these two antithetical forces. No drama of Ibsen's, not even *Ghosts*, produces a more devastating effect in the theater.

Indeed, *Ghosts* represents, in some degree, a withdrawal

from the abrupt, uncompromising position of *A Doll's House*. The attack upon the play as a play is muted in the later piece, though the second part of the drama attacks the first part just as ruthlessly as in *A Doll's House*. Within a framework provided by the action of completing the Captain Alving Memorial Orphanage, the premises of the first action are libertarian-idealist; Mrs. Alving asserts, against stuffy Parson Manders, the right of the free soul to read "advanced" books, to haunt Bohemian artistic circles in Paris, to contemplate with equanimity incest itself. And Parson Manders, because he is an impenetrable booby, reassures the audience that there is nothing to be feared from these scarecrows. The voice of fear is afraid of his own shadow; clearly, the other actors, good liberals that they are, have nothing to fear but fear itself. The strong common sense of Mrs. Alving enlists the sympathy of the audience in pooh-poohing the illiberal and obscurantist superstition that is afraid even to look at a fresh idea. But at the end of the first act a first crack appears in Mrs. Alving's bold façade; Oswald, the symbol of her new-found liberty, turns to repeating the behavior of his caged father. He is caged in his own inheritance. Thenceforth, as Mrs. Alving's libertarian determination to finish with the long, dreadful comedy of her hidden life grows ever stronger, the doom which is deeper and darker than even Parson Manders ever imagined keeps advancing over her. The action takes two opposed lines: the orphanage, which the audience has recognized all along as a whited sepulcher, burns up at the end of Act II; and Act III is devoted to the remorseless burning of Oswald, the free soul, the hero of the play's libertarian movement.

Ibsen is not, however, a simple libertarian; the doom of Mrs. Alving grows from a failure of self-recognition, and the drama, which at its close has narrowed down to so simple and terrible an act of choice, has really been concerned throughout with choosing and failing to choose. The point is old and familiar that Mrs. Alving is a Nora who stayed at home; more crucially, she is a Nora who did not choose, who tried with her pathetic orphanage to live the life of appearances and with her pathetic son to live the life of ethical freedom and self-realization. The demand which is made on her takes the form of "either-or"; the price of living with Captain Alving is a wormy son, the price of health is leaving Captain Alving, the price of trying to live two lives is to make a mess of both. As venereal disease destroys Mrs. Alving's dream of a bold free life for Oswald, the burning of the orphanage destroys her dream of covering up for the Captain. The point is not that she made a wrong decision in returning to her husband's bed; it is that, in the deeper sense, she never decided at all. She never accepted the Captain or an alternative to him, never chose to live ethically or conventionally, but paltered instead. Her punishment, almost Dantesque in its aptness, is to continue in a state of indecision indefinitely; and in that last harrowing scene where she stands over her idiot son tearing at her grey hairs and screaming in the agony of a bottomless indecision, the blackest implication is that by now it does not matter whether she decides anything or not.

Ghosts, then, makes no attack on the aesthetic delusion as such; its theme is indecisiveness, not choice, and it does not even accord to the point of view which one might call "aesthetic" the dignity of a three-dimensional representative. In Parson Manders the conventional aesthetic dolt whom we knew as Torvald Helmer reaches such depths of blockishness that he can undergo no further develop-

ment. He is repeated in minor roles as Rector Kroll or
Peter Stockmann; but prevailingly the burden of representing the aesthetic failure shifts hereafter to such Gyntian
figures as Hialmar Ekdal, Ulric Brendel, and Halvard Sol-
ness. *Ghosts* does not, to be sure, resolve its conflict after
the pattern of classical tragedy; for in Mrs. Alving we have
followed the growth of a morbid condition, not the defeat
of an endeavor which catches our sympathies in its culmination and crushing. The quality of the audience's sympathy
with Mrs. Alving has been sharply reduced by ironic commentary throughout the play, so that her ambition for the
free Oswald, which is the play's closest approach to an
active aspiration, is made to seem obsessive and unnatural
from beginning to end. One is not involved with her; she
is, rather, displayed as a specimen, an experiment. Consequently, the play ends, not with the protagonist (and,
in him, the audience) reduced to a state of rest, not with
a stasis and that acceptance of reality which follows a transfer and a purging, but with both protagonist and audience
wrung up to the highest pitch of blind anguish. Here the
play stops; and the audience departs, not purged but shaken,
not resolved but haunted.

From the Periclean point of view, Ibsen's dramatic art
in *A Doll's House* and *Ghosts* is nothing less than *coitus
interruptus* cruelly imposed by a perverse or blundering
playwright. Sensationalism, perversion, and mental degeneration were the mildest terms used during the 1890's by
Periclean critics to account for Ibsen's peculiar impact on
an audience in the theater.[2] Then, when it became clear

---

[2] For a more recent example of the Periclean assumptions applied
to an unfair contrast between Ibsen and Shakespeare, see J. W.
Krutch, *The Modern Temper* (Harvest Books), ch. v.

that he was not to be disposed of by open attack, the process of watering down began. The catch phrase "problem plays" gained currency; and by treating *A Doll's House* as an essay on women's rights and *Ghosts* as an essay on venereal disease, critics found it easy to evade the full force of their impact. But the essence of poetry for Ibsen (and he applied the term "poetry" deliberately to both these plays) was never simply discussion or exposition, never simply information or reform. Poetry existed to pass doom judgment on the human soul. And we do not do justice to the plays till we see them as expressing Ibsen's ultimate vision of the human condition. For, on Ibsen's terms, man is never in the right; the essence of being human is to be possessed of a bad conscience. The state of being anxious is more widespread and deep-rooted than the ideologies by which men attempt to explain it. As for the Periclean view of man, whole and harmonious, at ease with himself and his surroundings, exercising an enlightened and rational choice among alternatives and controlling his faculties—this view Ibsen rejected, sometimes explicitly, sometimes tacitly, as untrue to his experience. He cultivated guilt, felt it to be part of his function to do so, and sought out the guilt of society, not as a satirist standing above it, but because it confirmed his own. His plays assert that guilt, explore it, analyze it, do everything but assuage it.

Here, perhaps, is the sharpest point of difference between Ibsen and his pseudo-disciple Shaw. Although *Mrs. Warren's Profession* is a major exception, Shaw's plays are often built on the assumption that what the audience needs is a brisk workout on a moral exercycle; the play is an act of health, a stimulating mock combat. (Sometimes, as in *Pygmalion*, the mock warfare may be prolonged beyond the limits of the play proper into an epilogue which merely carries inconclusiveness one stage further; yet, as it continues, this conflict is resolved by diminution of its scale and intensity into a mere parlor game, a skirmish of familiar rhetorics.) For Ibsen, a play is a bitter delusion unless it leads us to recognize our own sickness to death. Thus Ibsen scorned the aesthetic, whereas a play like *Major Barbara*, even as it pretends to mock "useless" aestheticism, is actually built on it. There is not the least scrap or trace of "fine writing" in either *A Doll's House* or *Ghosts;* there is almost no plot, little invention, no wit or style, no surface attraction. Ibsen's plays build by the deepening of a conflict which goes beyond intention, a conflict which lies at the taproots of character. When it has been narrowed and deepened as much as possible, when we have reached absolute impasse, the play stops. This is reality; it kills, it destroys, it is impossible to endure—Ibsen throws it down before the audience and dares them to pick it up, to see for themselves, to deny, if they can, that this is the way things are. The audience have not followed the fortunes of the protagonist as their own; they have watched the working of a judgment which at the last minute expands, in the very process of evading a merely aesthetic resolution, to include the audience itself. Where the Sophoclean tragedy ends with a laying down of guilt by the audience, Ibsen's plays end with an assumption of guilt by the audience. Nora Helmer leaves the stage to find a less repulsive way of life elsewhere; the audience, which has found her way of life silly and generous and rather amusing on the whole, is left with its sloppy, undemanding standards, its guilt. *Ghosts*, less direct in making the audience responsible for the fate which overtakes its protagonists, nonetheless commits its audience in the first part of the play to an easy, sentimental admiration for libertarian ideals which the last act of the drama ruthlessly demolishes. The pattern in both plays is to involve the audience in sympathy for a program which is later attacked as unworthy or inadequate. Both actions are fully worked out in the formal sense, to a complete pattern; one could not want either play prolonged or shortened by a word or a gesture; but the impact of both on the audience is unresolved, since the plays do not lead to or aim at an emotional equilibrium, consequently do not aim at or accept an aesthetic definition of their effect. They aim at moving and disturbing the audience beyond the formal framework of the author-actor-audience relationship; and their structure is open in this longitudinal sense, that there is no apparent limit to the impact at which they aim. An open literary structure may thus be the expression of a closed philosophic structure which assigns to literature itself an inferior status. Such a literary work tries to surmount its categorical inferiority by a kinesis which grows out of the entrapment structure (the audience committed, then attacked), combined with a deliberate failure to close off the end of the pattern. This structure may aim at causing the work of art to overflow its aesthetic condition and to exist in an ethical, nonstructured capacity within the audience's mind; and so far as the plays of Ibsen's middle period are open in their structure, this is their peculiar quality. The caprice of *Peer Gynt*, the ritualistic formalism of *John Gabriel Borkman*, are more comfortable, more easily digestible extremes. Each in its own way represents a closed form, one free, one rigid, but both closed in the sense that their structure is consistent throughout and shaped toward the resolution of a single set of themes. Being of a piece, they are self-sufficient and tend to accept their aesthetic status. The middle plays accept no such placid estimate of themselves; and though demonstration is pretty much out of the question, the opinion may nonetheless be expressed that they are bigger and more exciting plays precisely because of their open structure.

A last wide speculation, to which one may attach as much or as little importance as one wants, is suggested by the odious reputation long born by Ibsen and the special relation of his plays to the theme of guilt. Thinking along Freudian lines, a psychologist has ventured to suggest a relation between literary form as such and relief from guilt. The work of art which resolves its problems and closes its form may be supposed to give a special sense of relief—not necessarily because any problem is solved in which one takes a practical interest, but because all structuring of life suggests a meaning for which any individual is only partly responsible, if at all. On these terms, the work in open form may represent a tribute to the reality principle and, perhaps more particularly, to the supreme form of that sinister impulse the death wish. An indirect corroboration of this view may be seen in a certain nihilism which marks Ibsen's later work, an almost monotonous addiction to the despairing, climactic suicide. To be sure, if guilt is as indefeasible as Ibsen supposes it, even suicide can represent only a symbolic absolution. Viewing the matter somewhat more mechanically, when resolution is impossible within the framework of human life, an ending must be sought outside it. From either point of view, Max Nordau was perfectly right; Ibsen in his character as author is the enemy not only of the people but of human existence itself. He was not joking when he spoke of wanting to "torpedo the Ark," nor was he playing devil's advocate either. He frequently saw human life as a sequence of follies and ineradicable corruptions in which the superior man merely found a quicker way to his own destruction. Death and marriage are typically used to end all sorts of dramatic conflicts; but suicide and willful separation are hallmarks of a complete and vindictive nihilism, to which works stressing unfinality seem sometimes addicted.

The paradox to which we are reduced is as big as life itself. If human existence involves at its core an instinct toward nonexistence, an appetite in no way secondary to the craving for life itself, what crime does the work of art commit that recognizes the death wish, builds upon its deep-laid position in the human heart, and re-enacts within its own theater the brutal, inconclusive experience of life in irrepressible conflict with its own assumptions? Of course one is always free to dismiss the death wish itself as an unproved hypothesis, of dubious necessity.

∿ IV ∿

Trompe-l'Oeil in Shakespeare and Keats

EMPHASIZING as they do the inferiority of aesthetic to ethical existence, the middle plays of Ibsen make use of open structure to call attention to, and denigrate, their own nature. So far as they are justified at all, the open structures of these plays are justified on expressive grounds; the device is appropriate to the attitude being expressed by the author and the structure of feelings being invoked in the reader or audience. Individual isolation is a keystone of this emotional structure; various relations have been suggested to the themes of personal guilt, a reality principle, and the death wish.

But many of Shakespeare's late plays seem to make use of an analogous structure for a quite contrary purpose. By deliberately overstepping the boundary between the aesthetic sphere and that of "real life," they seek to convince us, not that the aesthetic is fraudulent, but that it is more real than reality itself; and this use of the device suggests certain relations, of contrast as well as similarity, with the work of Keats among the romantic poets. A basic common motif is that which may be described, by analogy with a device long familiar in the graphic arts, under the name of *trompe-l'oeil*.

By means of *trompe-l'oeil* the artist mingles and contrasts different levels of representation. Within the frame of a still life there may occur, fastened to the surface of the canvas, a literal jackknife or a prosaic pencil. A figure painted within a frame may be depicted as reaching across the frame to claim existence in a third dimension. A statue which is stepping off its pedestal or a *putto* who supports a framing drape yet takes part in the picture framed exemplifies *trompe-l'oeil*. Or a series of receding frames may be depicted, as for instance in a picture of a man looking at a painting of a room with a window opening on a landscape; and if, let us say, the sun shining through this painting of a painted window illuminates the face of the painted looker-on, the whole image may be called *trompe-l'oeil*. A pair of gloves painted as hanging over a doorknob, a painted hand reaching around a painted doorway and holding a painted towel—here are further examples. The device is essentially that of the overstepped or obliterated frame; its effect is to surprise by the incongruity or to impress by the depth of representational levels; and though less frequent in literature than in the plastic arts, it does have an existence on the printed page.

The usual effect of literary *trompe-l'oeil* is for comedy or burlesque; its usual setting is the drama. A classic English example, extraordinary only in its completeness, is *The Knight of the Burning Pestle*, which blocks out the water-color sentiments of a bourgeois comedy with the broad, blunt audience-figures of George the Grocer, Mistress Nell, and prentice Ralph. Before so weak a background, they stand out in the strong, unchallenged shades of burlesque. George and Nell are themselves a new frame. They intrude occasionally upon the action to fortify Ralph or pet a child; but in general they simply comment at the beginnings and ends of scenes, while Ralph performs those violations of the inner play which constitute the typical action of the piece. This action is a physical as well as a mental intrusion of the audience upon the stage, and a comparatively mechanical intrusion at that. Ralph's speeches are separate, and his actions are mostly unobserved by and irrelevant to the actors of the inner play. Beaten by Jasper in Act II, he is quite driven out of the plot and thenceforth goes his own way, revenging himself on the barber in Act III, being transported to Moldavia in Act IV, and exercising the trainbands in Act V. " 'Tis long of yourself, sir," the Boy very sensibly tells George, "we have nothing to do with his part." But the separation is functional after all; for the wit of the piece lies in the fact that the inner play is itself a bourgeois play, fantastic indeed, but still too bourgeois for the bourgeoisie. Hence, while the inner play mirrors the prosaic fantasies of bourgeois life (honest prentice Jasper marries the boss's daughter), the outer play portrays as in dream sequence the secret life, heroic and fragmentary, of the London middle class. The reality which climbs up on the stage out of the pit, so the play tells us, is more imaginary than the sober imaginings of poets. But both are ridiculous; and honest old Merrythought, who rolls uproariously through the drama from one end to the other, holds Ralph and Venturewell as equally absurd. As absurd and as fantastic, the simple-minded bourgeois is thus set at a double distance. The eye which is deceived belongs to George, not to the actual audience or to Merrythought or to the poet; and in fact the whole pathetic delusion could scarcely be more strongly reprobated. Only fools like George, Ralph, and Nell are taken in by stage pretense.

Looking back to Cervantes and ahead to Ludvig Tieck —being, as it were, pregnant with Pirandello's *Six Characters in Search of an Author* and instinct with that burlesque spirit which only a hair separates from tragicomedy, *The Knight of the Burning Pestle* may serve as a sort of norm, a plain, sensible base line in the handling of *trompe-l'oeil*. For while accepting the stage as fraud, and conventional fraud at that, it attacks fantasy as preposterous and thus takes as its supreme value a sort of plain common sense that creates illusions only to destroy them and blows bubbles to watch them burst.

Cervantes himself was far more equivocal; and Shakespeare typically destroys obvious illusions in order to create deeper ones. So it is in *Hamlet*. The Prince, seeing the working of a player's fictional passion, falls into one which we are to suppose real; and the contrast of aesthetic artifice and ethical reality suggests to him the "Mouse-Trap" as a conscience-catching device. In the scene and soliloquy centering about the Pyrrhus speech, however, it is not a reality which intrudes upon and mocks an artifice, but an artifice which intrudes upon an ethical reality, reflecting back the mockery directed against it by providing scope for the action of the mocker. Thus the factitious blank verse which is normal to the play must be heightened to bombast in the players; and the intruding locution has the effect of a foil, against which the facets of the play proper are made to glitter more brightly.

But there are other, subtler forms of violated context than this, in which the actual outlines of "artificial" art, "natural" character, and flesh-and-blood audience are con-

fused. In a most striking passage, Cleopatra as she takes
on immortal longings pauses a moment to describe for Iras
the play in which they have been taking part.

> Thou, an Egyptian puppet, shalt be shown
> In Rome as well as I. Mechanic slaves,
> With greasy aprons, rules, and hammers, shall
> Uplift us to the view. In their thick breaths,
> Rank of gross diet, shall we be enclouded,
> And forc'd to drink their vapour. . . .
> > Saucy lictors
> Will catch at us like strumpets, and scald rhymers
> Ballad us out o'tune. The quick comedians
> Extemporally will stage us and present
> Our Alexandrian revels. Antony
> Shall be brought drunken forth, and I shall see
> Some squeaking Cleopatra boy my greatness
> I' th' posture of a whore.

The words, of course, describe the play itself, which is
now all but completed; they are spoken by a boy to an
audience that has seen Alexandrian revels in Act I and
drunken Antony in Act II. Their effect is to withdraw
and conceal; what the members of the audience have seen,
greasy mechanic fellows that they are, is but a low image
of more splendid reality. Antony and Cleopatra have been
made a motley to the view, but behind the play itself,
which they denounce as aesthetic and cheap, they proclaim a superaesthetic reality which is presumed precious.
The passage turns against the audience the sharp edge of
a vindictiveness that has been implicit in the play's whole
theme, the contrast between a dream life which is real and
a public life which is shadow.

Cleo. Think you there was or might be such a man
     As this I dreamt of?
Dol. Gentle madam, no.
Cleo. You lie, up to the hearing of the gods!
     But, if there be or ever were one such,
     It's past the size of dreaming. Nature wants stuff
     To vie strange forms with fancy; yet, t'imagine
     An Antony were nature's piece 'gainst fancy,
     Condemning shadows quite.

The speech involves a play on *nature*. The vision of Antony
which Cleopatra can see and Dolabella cannot must be for
her more than a fantasy. Although it outrages, *because* it
outrages common sense, it must be part of her. Outside
nature (Dolabella's nature) indeed wants stuff to vie with
inner fancy, so the latter must be mistrusted; but to imagine
an Antony is an act of defiance on the part of one's inner
nature and against the fancy that flatters outside nature.
If there neither was in outside nature nor might be (in
dreaming) such a man, then inner nature must image him
forth; and to do so is that nature's revenge upon fancy, a
new light which condemns shadows of every sort. The
shadows which Shakespeare's audience has before it are
then but the shadows of shadows; while the real radiance
of the characters is deliberately withdrawn into the inner
essence of their imagined selves.

    Shakespeare violates the aesthetic frame by calling at-
tention to it in order to belittle the aesthetic act and thereby
create the effects of depth and distance. What intrudes
upon the play itself is something more real and glamorous
than the play, a vision of personality created for the audience by being taken away from it, and presented by being

withdrawn. The device is subject to ever more complex embroidery in the later plays and is more and more elusively used. The very title of *The Winter's Tale* cries down a fable that, so long as it pretends to significance has none, but as soon as it becomes a rural charade attracts the poet's loving interest.

These your unusual weeds to each part of you [says Florizel]
Do give a life.

They do indeed. As Polixenes, heretofore placid to the point of dullness, discourses with Perdita on carnations and gilliflowers, he suddenly blossoms into a speech, cribbed from Puttenham, about art and nature; and what he says makes multiple reference to the play itself and to the several frames which surround it.

> Nature is made better by no mean,
> But Nature makes that mean; so, over that art
> Which you say adds to Nature, is an art
> That Nature makes. You see, sweet maid, we marry
> A gentler scion to the wildest stock,
> And make conceive a bark of baser kind
> By bud of nobler race. This is an art
> Which does mend nature, change it rather, but
> The art itself is Nature.

The grafting image of course implies ironic half-reference to the marriage in prospect between Florizel and Perdita; but the play itself and the sheepshearing scene particularly are gentler grafts on a ruder fable. The speech as a whole makes reference to the pastoral mode by which noble impulses are grafted upon rural manners and to this play in particular, which is utterly artificial but in this, its moment of highest artifice, betrays a nature greater than itself. Yet Shakespeare no sooner offers this idea of art as natural and therefore trustworthy than, in the ragged person of Autolycus the balladmonger, he withdraws it. As this personage is announced, a solemn, simple disjointed discussion starts between Dorcas, Mopsa, and the Clown which evidently parodies the Shakespearean audience as Shakespeare saw it.

"I love a ballad but even too well," says the Clown, "if it be doleful matter merrily set down, or a very pleasant thing indeed and sung lamentably."

"I love a ballad in print o' life," echoes Mopsa, "for then we are sure they are true"; and she joins with Dorcas in anxious queries as to whether all the songs are true. Autolycus reassures them solemnly enough and meanwhile picks purses to his heart's content. In addition to his balladmongering, he is a thief, a mimer, and a thriving observer of highways and byways, with a fine feeling for his character as a rogue. Standing altogether outside the plot, mocking everyone in it as he helps it on, and suggesting through his namesake a talent for flimflam transformation, he may be fairly identified with the capricious Shakespearean fancy. The Clown, who is, as it were, the audience, "wants but something to be a reasonable man"; and Autolycus, who is, as it were, the poet, wants a good deal to be an honest one. The play itself is thus reduced to an odd sort of commerce indeed. Only the miracle of Perdita, whom the plot manages to lose and find, to make a princess, a shepherdess, and a princess again without degrading the brightness of her perceptions or the fantastic buoyant elaboration of her wit—only Perdita seems to excite the poet's mind and style. And her brilliance is not merely independent of the plot; it is enhanced by Shakespeare's mockery of that humble mechanical item.

A last and famous example of *trompe-l'oeil*, through which Shakespeare places his whole career in new perspective, is from *The Tempest*. The two speeches of Prospero (IV, i; V, i), dismissing the revels and abjuring his art, make direct reference to the fantasy of the play itself in order to equate it with the fantasy of life.

> We are such stuff
> As dreams are made on, and our little life
> Is rounded with a sleep.

The "we" here is a limitless word; it is spoken at once of a fantasy within a fantasy and of the prosaic admission-paying audience. Above all it concerns the poet himself, whom one senses above and beyond the situation of players and audience, beyond the contrast of fantasy and common sense. As he equates and dismisses the revels, the audience, and the whole pageant of life, the poet thus reveals and withdraws himself and by the remoteness of his perspective (from which all life seems tiny and complete) suggests the intensity of a new vision. Of a piece with his putting off of worldly display is Prospero's breaking his staff and drowning his books. Even Caliban knows that books alone distinguish master from servant;

> Remember
> First to possess his books; for without them
> He's but a sot, as I am.

This power is further amplified by Prospero in words that apply only remotely, if at all, to the character's career, and very directly to Shakespeare's own:

> graves at my command
> Have wak'd their sleepers, op'd, and let 'em forth
> By my so potent art.

Thus, discarding his artificial but personal talent and resuming his natural but social rank, he retires to a remote Milan next door to the deeper remoteness of the grave, whence the aesthetic delusion of the play, the shows of worldly power, and the very illusion of everyday solidity all appear equally baseless.

Of the five levels of reality reference in *The Tempest*,[1] the revels within the play are most transparent. But as Shakespeare leads us through ever-deeper veils of illusion toward an ultimate truth which is itself imaginary, the second level we leave behind is the play itself and the next is that everyday, prosaic common sense in which *The Knight of the Burning Pestle* had placed its perfect confidence.

Does the total effect add up to that of an "open" form? The more literally we define "form," the less closed the plays seem to be. Their unity is, if anything, cyclical; through the play itself we get a glimpse of the poetic imagination; and, seen by the eye of imagination, even the wretched stage play which introduced us to it may be transfigured. Duke Theseus does not hesitate to say of the silliest stuff ever put on stage, "The best in this kind are but shadows; and the worst are no worse, if imagination amend them." Thus, the form is open in that the playwright appeals to a principle outside the play to justify its final unity;

---

[1] They may be listed, working, as it were, from the kernel out, as (1) the revels, (2) *The Tempest*, (3) the audience in London at Whitehall, (4) Milan identified with Stratford and the kingdom of Shakespeare's mind, and (5) eternity.

on the other hand, the vision which engulfs, and dwarfs, the play is itself unitary. Shakespeare works here with a special variation of that ironic openness which derives from juxtaposing the several incompatible points of view made possible by a hierarchic universe; we shall see a notable variation of it in Cervantes. But its final effect, unlike that of Cervantes' novel, is encompassing, pervasive, and unitary. Precisely because the highest unity which literature can achieve is imaginary, there is no vindictiveness to Shakespeare's denigration of stage machinery. His "openness," such as it is, stands apart from that which we have previously examined as a more genially motivated device for fracturing the aesthetic in order to enhance the imaginative structure of reference.

Much as Shakespeare refined and turned to literary ends a device that his contemporaries used mostly for burlesque purposes, so Keats is distinguished among the romantic poets by the revelatory use of recessed, overstepped frames. But the frames are fewer and the contrasts, though sometimes more poignant, sometimes simply more bitter, are manipulated by a hand less serene and secure. A first example, from almost the end of Keats's brief career, strikes rather heavily, but apparently with serious intent, the same note as Beaumont sounded humorously. In the middle of "Lamia" Keats turns directly on his own verses and criticizes them from the standpoint of literal, commonplace reality:

> Let the mad poets say whate'er they please
> Of the sweets of Faeries, Peris, Goddesses,
> There is not such a treat among them all,
> Haunters of cavern, lake, and waterfall,

> As a real woman, lineal indeed
> From Pyrrha's pebbles or old Adam's seed.

The eloquence here is rather edible, in the style of Leigh Hunt; a lady praised as "a real woman" could scarcely help feeling like a fine joint of meat, as Fanny Brawne apparently rather uncomfortably did. The reader too is taken aback at being presented with such a physical commodity; and the truly delicate balance maintained in the poem between Lamia as snake and Lamia as woman is in danger of being upset. It appears that she was woman before she became snake (I, 117) and the snake's body was a prison house to her (I, 203); yet the poet nowhere tells us whether Hermes enchanted a snake into the form of a woman or disenchanted a woman from the form of a snake. To "cold philosophy" Lamia is nothing but a cold snake; to Lycius she is a bride so warmly splendid that to be deprived of her destroys him. The aesthetic delusion is then a delusion and perhaps, as Apollonius says without contradiction, a fatal one; but to be without it is to cease to exist. Between these troubling but lofty alternatives the "real woman" loses both stature and function; we could gladly be without her.

But the odes, which keep meat-and-potatoes reality at a fair aesthetic remove, are more successful in handling the device of frames overstepped. Their typical structure is that of a vision in a dream, of a discovery made by the mind upon itself. The "Ode to Psyche," for instance, opens with an apology that a poem about the psyche should be directed to her:

> And pardon that thy secrets should be sung
> Even into thine own soft-conched ear.

Personified Psyche is next discovered within a forest; she is a deity without temple or prophet, who has never had temple or prophet. But though modern times are "far retired / From happy pieties," Keats can even now see and believe and draw inspiration from Psyche:

> I see, and sing, by my own eyes inspir'd.

He is inspired, that is, by what he has seen of his own psyche in his own imagination, to which he directs his song; the forest in which Psyche has been found sleeping is at once identified with the wilderness of the mind, and her proper habitat with the deepest recesses of it:

> Yes, I will be thy priest, and build a fane
> In some untrodden region of my mind.

Here, surrounded by branched thoughts, by the wreathed trellis of a working brain, by the soft delights of shadowy thoughts, and by the multitudinous flowers of Fancy's breeding, will be the sanctuary; and within this deepest arcanum,

> A bright torch, and a casement ope at night
> To let the warm Love in.

We thus have nestled within one another like a series of Chinese boxes the poet's public exterior life, within which appears a dreamlike vision of Psyche, from which the poet retreats to a new and untrodden region of his mind, at the heart of which he builds a fane, with an inner room. But one word of the last eloquent stanza cuts across all these walls and divisions. Keats will dress his sanctuary

> With all the gardener Fancy e'er could feign,

and this *feigning* (the pun is altogether odd) carries a judgment from the outermost box of all into the heart of the imagination and reminds us that the sensible exterior world has a word, and a rather crushing word, to say against this intense imaginative experience. Nothing like this appears in the little poem "Fancy" in which Keats first (December, 1818) apostrophized his own mind. Its appearance in the "Psyche" ode shows Keats led toward a deepening awareness of fancy as a separate mode of experience and toward a steadily heightened dramatic use of overstepped frames in the great poems. The word "feign" is passed over in the "Ode to Psyche" without further comment; but it is close kin to two other pejorative intrusive verbs in two of the greatest odes: to "cheat" in the "Ode to a Nightingale" and to "tease" in the "Ode on a Grecian Urn." For the moment let us notice only the special direction in which Keats oversteps his frames. For while Shakespeare carried us from aesthetic illusion to something more solid, brilliant, or comprehensive beyond it, Keats recedes deeper and deeper into it and is rescued or destroyed (the ambiguity is unresolved) by something cold and reasonable outside it. For Shakespeare imagination is the empyrean, for Keats it is the very pit of psychology.

Receding is, indeed, the special metier of Keats; the "Ode to a Nightingale" opens with an emphasized and re-emphasized "fading" into the experience of the song and into the forest of the mind. At the heart of this forest in the sanctuary of sensation Keats finds an embalmed darkness, a darkness at once soothing and mortuary; and the experience suggests a still further withdrawal, to the rich regions of death. Intimate though the association evidently is in Keats's mind, one cannot help feeling the extension from aesthetic passivity to death itself (stanza 6 of the poem) as something of a structural digression, perhaps an

anticipation of the "Grecian Urn" themes. The hard cold-
ness of death cannot be absent from one's richest dreams
of it; and the experience which Keats is now celebrating
is one of unalloyed richness and depth. Elysium is of course
a region

> Where the nightingale doth sing
> Not a senseless, tranced thing,
> But divine melodious truth;
> Philosophic numbers smooth.

But this is not Elysium, it is death; and we must be rescued
from its chill finality by a graceful but formal antithesis.
Although the person dies, the song as an aesthetic experience lives as it has always lived, within, but untouched by,
the hungry generations of men. In the estranged heart of
Ruth it once revived memories of home, and in the universal heart it has ofttimes charmed open casements looking into magic landscapes, landscapes which are both
"faery" and "forlorn." These two adjectives come together
(one might say "collide") at the very heart of the poem,
when we have faded into the mind's forest, into the further
remoteness of ancient grief, and then into the landscape
beyond the innermost casements of the mind. But the intruding word "forlorn" is not here passed over; so far as
the aesthetic-death passage can be redeemed, it is now
justified by the "forlorn," which tolls Keats back from a
world of life with the bird to a world of death in his sole
self. The contrast is completed, but only as hyperbole;
there is a death of the body in the aesthetic sphere, as there
is a death of the spirit in the here and now,

> Where palsy shakes a few, sad, last gray hairs,
> Where youth grows pale, and spectre-thin, and dies.

And in the shock of adjusting to the new sphere, Keats denounces the old one in words which tend to mislead:

> Adieu! the fancy cannot cheat so well
> As she is fam'd to do, deceiving elf.

It may be that if we accept these lines as the core of the poem, if we suppose that the experiences described in stanzas 4 through 7 are a mere cheat and deception, if we assume that the central experience of the poem is a "revery" which is now discovered to be false, then the poet has not made enough of his discovery and may properly be accused of lacking ironic insight into his plight, as Brooks and Warren have in fact accused him. But the poet has been "tolled" back to this viewpoint. He has suffered a death; and the last two lines of the poem, because they phrase the question in less hyperbolic terms, ask more explicitly than ever which area of experience was "real":

> Was it a vision or a waking dream?
> Fled is that music:—Do I wake or sleep?

Rueful irony might be appropriate enough, might even be necessary, if Keats knew he had been daydreaming. He does not, nor if one reads him with any sympathy, does the reader. What he has experienced, though not of the here and now, has its own imaginative reality, its truth to the mind which knows it. The poem is a statement, not of unity within reality (as R. H. Fogle argues in *The Imagery of Keats and Shelley*), but of diversity among realities. The spheres of our being are ultimately incongruous; and while we may progress through them to the inmost kernel of each, the experience of each is not only partial in itself but destructive of other orders of experience. To be deluded by Lamia is fatal, as she is a serpent; but to be enlightened

by bald-headed Apollonius is fatal too. Conceivable resolutions of this dilemma on the philosophic plane lie in making its intensity or its variety or both these qualities the
value of any experience, as in *Man and Superman*, Act III;
for the present purpose it suffices to note that Keats has
combined with special dramatic power the uses made by
both Beaumont and Shakespeare of *trompe-l'oeil*. As he
recesses his imaginative frames to show the shoddiness of
the everyday he intrudes a dramatic final word to show the
frailty of the imaginative sphere.

The "Ode on a Grecian Urn" compresses these themes
and schemes still further. This poem begins by apostrophiz-
ing and interrogating the urn as a shape seen at a distance.
Stanza 2 moves our viewpoint, subtly enough, to within
the urn; we are now in a position to hear, as the dancing
figures hear, the unheard music of the pipes and to formu-
late for a lover within the urn a tentative balance of gains
and losses:

> She cannot fade, though thou hast not thy bliss.

The next two stanzas (3 and 4) are occupied with the
elaboration of this contrast, the poem reaching something
like a climax with Keats's favorite empathy word, "warm":

> For ever warm and still to be enjoy'd,
> For ever panting, and for ever young.

But this is no climax comparable to stanza 7 of the
"Nightingale" ode; we have not moved far from the surface of things (one frame only has been recessed), and
the poetry is relatively thoughtful and undisturbed. The
fourth stanza slopes to a conclusion through a quietly de-
clining series of adjectives: the little town, first peaceful,
then falls silent, and is at last desolate.

Returning to its original attitude of apostrophe from out-side, the poem addresses in the fifth and final stanza a re-proach to the urn. A silent form, it "teases" us out of thought as does eternity; and while eternity suggests a truthfulness more than human, "teasing" implies a down-right deception. The omens are thus balanced: art is eternal, but it is not true; it is a higher form of truth, but we must be teased into it and cannot remain long under its influence. In stanza 3 the poet *was* thus teased out of thought; but in stanza 5 he clearly is not. And as "cold philosophy" en-abled or forced Apollonius to see Lamia as a cold-blooded snake, so now the fact that the poet is no longer teased out of thought enables or forces him to see the urn as a "cold pastoral." This muscular image clearly shows the poet within the realm of thought and time and aware of wast-age and woe as the urn in its cold, formal eternity cannot be. That the poet should from this point of view foresee the urn's unchanged survival, its eternal murmuring of an unchanging message to changing man, is nothing sur-prising. A sylvan historian would naturally have some such function. The message itself strikes us more oddly, though only a little more so. The urn, which is unalterably of the aesthetic sphere, should not and could not speak to us in the common-sense language of men. What it says, then, is spoken from its special point of view; and within that sphere all that is beautiful is real. So far we have not burst the bounds of orthodox neo-Platonism. But the last line and a half of the poem,

> that is all
> Ye know on earth, and all ye need to know.

—these lines pose a sizable problem. Are we to take them, in the first place, as the comment of the urn or of Keats?

More cogent yet, to whom are they addressed? A textual confusion may throw a bit of light here. Keats's manuscript and three transcripts of it place only a comma and dash in the penultimate line,

> Beauty is truth, truth beauty,—that is all. . . .

But the magazine text of January 1820 alters the comma to a period, and the text published in volume form (June 1820) adds inverted commas around "Beauty is truth, truth beauty." Keats's tendency is thus to separate by increasingly high barriers the urn's motto from the last line and a half of the poem. If this line and a half are not spoken on the same level as what precedes them, need they be supposed the words of the urn at all? Perhaps, as the position of the closing quote suggests, we are to imagine Keats speaking them. But if we suppose them addressed (whether by the urn or by Keats) to the human beings of stanza 5 and not to the eternally happy artifacts of stanza 3, they are obviously untrue, incongruous with Keats's philosophy elsewhere expressed, and inappropriate to the theme and structure of this very poem. If they are spoken by the urn to men, but with a tacit limitation so that we are to sense them as ironically partial, that interpretation (persuasively championed by C. M. Bowra in *The Romantic Imagination*) is conceivable, though strained by the necessity of inventing the limitation. But perhaps the last words of the poem are not spoken *by* but *to* the urn and the figures on it. The emphasis is then on the "ye's," which, if they cannot be directed to the singular urn (Keats does not, within the limits of my observation, use "ye" as a singular form), may be directed to the figures on the urn. The force of the passage is then vindictive; "It's enough for *you* to say, 'truth and beauty are the same'—that's your function in the world. But we who are men know this and something else too." Whether or not the passage will bear this sense, the poem's closing remark is clearly intended in the aesthetic sphere; it teases us into and out of thought, and in the very act of declaring our alienation from the sphere of the urn, translates us into it.

Odd though it seems at first, the use which Keats makes of open form is rather closer to that of Ibsen than to that of Shakespeare. He represents the vindictive and inconclusive opposition of imagination and reality, rather than their mutual illumination. His patterns are often those of total indecision and defeat, as evidenced by the tendency of his poems to bend back on themselves, in rondo form, with the poet having passed through a central vision only to come out where he went in, or a little further back. Whether the imagined experience or the return to reality or the incompatibility of the two is responsible, death is persistently associated with the cycle, as it scarcely is with the Shakespearean imagination. The moral theme observed in Euripides and Ibsen is missing, however; Keats never tries to imply that it is wrong to seek aesthetic gratification. Indeed, his total indifference to moral considerations is a refreshing peculiarity among the English poets, and he never invokes death as a penalty for aesthetic, social, or intellectual daring. More often, it is a dramatic convenience, a way of underlining disparity and cutting off cyclical repetition, or a supreme experience sought for its own sake. The cycle form is frequent in Keats, mechanical narrative unity serving here, as it often does elsewhere, to structure philosophic diversity and intellectual irresolution. Although both poets are much occupied with death as completion, for Shakespeare noble death is a last magnificent mirroring of one's self-image, while for Keats it is luxurious self-surrender. Keats calls attention to his writing as writing in order to emphasize that it is a comfortable fraud, and only partial and temporary and perhaps not very comfortable at that; Shakespeare, far more consistently, derogates the mechanical appendages of plot, play, players, and so on in order to deepen our wonder at the mind which lies behind (and yet includes) them. Shakespeare's vision is ultimately unitary; Keats's is not. Thus Keats's feeling for death betrays a sharper and more vindictive reaction to life than one typically notes in Shakespeare; and the association of unresolved conflict, ego-division, death wish, and open form is once again apparent. One may well wonder if there is any escape from this disturbing correlation. Between burlesque and morbidity, does the open form have any significant uses? Can it, for example, be turned to limited comic or simply serious ends? Cervantes is a hopeful place to look for positive answers to these questions.

∽ V ∽

Two Lines from Cervantes

NO OBSERVATION about *Don Quixote* is less startling than that the novel is built around an unresolved tension between Don Quixote's world and Sancho Panza's. These are, in the despairing oversimplifications of literary criticism, the world of imagination and that of appetite. Don Quixote makes his forays into the world of appetite and is brutally or comically rebuffed; the world of appetite makes counter-forays into Don Quixote's imagination and meets with a resistance just as stout and determined. One line of comic tension in the novel is drawn by Don Quixote's continual teetering on the edge of sanity. He can be led so far down a logical path toward the recognition of his own delusion that escape seems impossible—yet escape he does, each time by a fresh stratagem. Some sort of subtle membrane shields his "madness"; blows, we quickly realize, will never pierce it, but ideas may, and they are more and more craftily insinuated into the texture of his thinking. But in order to sink their shafts, the exponents of common sense must adopt the manners of the knight's delusion and enter into his masquerade. Bachelor Sampson becomes suc-

cessively the Knight of the Mirrors and the Knight of the
White Moon—his aim, in both guises, being to reflect
Quixote's real madness from his own feigned chivalry,
to vanquish him in imagination and so send him home to
the world of appetite. He succeeds in this enterprise of
degradation, but only at the end of the book and only over
the protests of the reader, whose sentiments are eloquently
voiced in the story itself by Don Antonio Moreno.

"Oh, sir," said Don Antonio, "may God pardon you the injury
you have done the whole world in your attempt to restore the
most amusing of all madmen to his senses. Don't you see, sir,
that no benefit to be derived from Don Quixote's recovery
could outweigh the pleasure afforded by his extravagances?
. . . And if it were not a sin against charity, I should say that I
hope Don Quixote may never be cured, for with his recovery
we not only should lose his pleasantries but his squire Sancho
Panza's as well" [ch. lxv].

Imagination is equated with delusion but also, sometimes, with a higher form of truth; in both capacities it
has immense power to influence the mind, so that the reasonable man can often be reached by the imaginative man,
when the imaginative man is quite beyond touch of the
reasonable one. An interesting early analogue is from Ben
Jonson. "Do you take me for an Amadis de Gaul or a Don
Quixote?" cries Kastril, the Angry Boy of *The Alchemist*.
The words are spoken just as the other dupes are being
carried by their folly beyond the reach of Surly's reasonable exposure. Folly and error animate them far more effectively than reason and the truth. Indeed, so far as Surly
relies merely on exposing the truth, he is totally ineffectual in the play, failing with Lovewit and Dame Pliant as
he fails against Face and Subtle—speaking what the prag-

matic, Aristotelian audience knows to be truth, what the rogues themselves have confessed to be truth, but finding it wholly ineffectual in the teeth of a persistent delusion.

Don Quixote is less definite about where truth really lies; what it opposes to Sancho's common sense is not merely roguery, appetite, and folly but a kind of divine wisdom inextricably mixed with folly, while in the person of Sancho roguery maintains a similar uneasy alliance with pragmatic reality. The long, leisurely, intimate quarrel of Quixote and Panza, in the course of which each assumes the manners and occasionally the position of the other, is the core of Cervantes' novel. Because he is solitary, active, misunderstood, and more capacious of understanding (as well as more entertaining) than anyone else in the book, our sympathies are generally with Don Quixote. But there is no ironclad rule about this; and in at least one incident Cervantes seems to go out of his way to show Don Quixote's brutality and indifference to human suffering. The boy Andrew who is rescued from his master's beating only to be beaten more ferociously than ever when Don Quixote's back is turned goes off swearing to find the knight and report his ill-treatment. He does so but is met with a curious lack of sympathy. The knight is embroiled at this point with Dorothea and Cardenio; he can spare Andrew only a vague promise of future vengeance. Andrew declares with some energy that he has no use for vengeance, present or future; he has been in the hospital as a result of his beating and is on his way to Seville to get another job. He needs neither vows nor vengeance nor knight-errantry in any of its forms, but something to eat and perhaps some money. There is general embarrassment in the face of this perfectly wretched, perfectly natural request; but only Sancho Panza does something about it. He gives the miserable Andrew a piece of bread and cheese—cold comfort enough—and as he departs, the unfortunate fellow cries, with understandable emphasis, "God blast you and every knight errant ever born on the face of the earth!" There is a harshness about this reprobation of Don Quixote, an austerity in the recognition that God's justice picks its own time, place, and person, which is typical of Cervantes' very Spanish blending of cruelty and sentiment.

Broadly speaking, the texture of the novel tends to avoid the middle area of flesh and blood: cities, homes, domestic experience, middle-class life in general. The landscape is stony, barren, dry; yet in the haze and clouds which overhang it all sorts of tremendous phantasms hover. The rock and the cloud: one wavers between these two aspects of reality, as the pilgrimage itself wavers between the knowledge that, for the more or less general purposes of Sancho, Aldonza Lorenzo is a country wench, while for the limited purposes of Don Quixote she is the Lady Dulcinea. This alternately hard and hazy landscape is a natural fact; it is also an influence, which blurs the outlines of even the most self-assured of Aristotelian moderates. The Knight of the Green Coat is such an Aristotelian moderate, who announces himself and rattles off his characteristics in the truly formidable terms of medieval allegory:

I am more than moderately rich, and my name is Don Diego de Miranda. I spend my life with my wife, my children, and my friends. My pursuits are hunting and fishing, though I keep neither hawk nor hounds, but only a quiet pointer and a good ferret or two. I have about six dozen books, some in Spanish, some in Latin. . . . I read profane books more than devotional.

. . . Sometimes I dine with my neighbors and friends. . . . My fare is good and well served [ch. xvii].

Sancho thinks these the words of a saint, and he actually falls down and worships this truly moderate man; but the scene is dramatic and loaded with moral comment both on Sancho and on the sensible gentleman. Given a prudential, appetitive world, this is, indeed, about as good as one can do; but there are other worlds. And in the adventure with the lions Cervantes spells the whole thing out by showing that one man's prudence may be another man's pusillanimity. "Pray go away, my dear sir," cries Don Quixote, not without a touch of contempt, "and see to your quiet pointer and your good ferret, and leave every man to do his duty. This is mine." He is not himself completely immoderate in this matter of courage; having provoked the first lion, he does not pursue him or undertake the second. But he does draw the lines between cowardice, courage, and foolhardiness as befits a knight-errant, whose calling is rather special —in a manner which clearly appeals to the moderate man as foolhardiness itself.

The point culminates in no simple relativism, such as an observation that the world looks one way to Sancho and the Green Knight, another way to Quixote. A distinct moral superiority is given to Quixote, if only by the circumstance that his view envelops and controls that of the appetitive characters. They have no recourse against him save the monotonous declaration that he is mad, salved by the shamefaced admission that he is entertaining. But he engulfs them by understanding and then dismissing their prudential motives. An uneasy, greasy dualism enables them to make the distinctions of this world for the purposes of this world, while reserving for the next world that loftier egalitarianism taught by Christ. Don Quixote is the same man here and there; and in a passage equally remarkable for its brilliance and its triteness he and Sancho combine to distinguish the two outlooks.

"Now tell me," says the Don, in his best lecture-tone, "have not you seen a play acted with Kings, Emperors, and Popes, knights, ladies, and various other personages brought on to the stage? One plays the ruffian, another the cheat; here is a merchant, there is a soldier; one is the wise fool, another the foolish lover. But when the play is over, and they have taken off their dresses, all the actors are equal."

"Yes, I have indeed," replied Sancho.

"Now the same thing," said Don Quixote, "happens in the comedy and traffic of this world, where some play Emperors, others Popes, and, in fact, every part that can be introduced into a play. But when we come to the end, which is when life is over, Death strips them of all the robes that distinguished them, and they are all equals in the grave" [ch. xii].

And Sancho goes on to compare life to a game of chess, where each piece has its value while the game continues but all are shuffled off, when the play is over, into a black leather bag, which is death.

Heaven is in fact a pattern of egalitarianism, of which poetry, pastoral life, and knight-errantry are in this world mere shadowy adumbrations. Don Quixote brings to the world, and finds in it, all sorts and levels of equality, from the hardships and adventures that bind together knight and squire to the pastoral simplicity of goatherds and the unscrupulous equality of lovers. In a thousand different ways Cervantes' book toys with the paradox of the Divine

Simpleton, who, because he knows nothing of the world's complexities, is all the more fitted to bring Christ's simplicity to the absurd, the hopeless test of action and practice.

Don Quixote can be read, then, as least in parts, at so exalted a level that its protagonist appears as the supreme exponent of that Christian wisdom which is worldly folly and his pilgrimage through Spain as a protracted Calvary. Perhaps there is no beatific vision; but the concept of heavenly peace as the ultimate objective of earthly warfare, a concept earnestly enforced in the discourse on arms and learning, is so evidently related to Don Quixote's behavior and so intimately related to the Christian scheme of things (laid out for all to see in Book xix of *The City of God*) as to make Cervantes' conscious purpose all but explicit. Don Quixote is not a Christ; simply, he takes the Christian injunctions literally and tries to put them into practice; he tries to love the galley slaves as he does himself. At heart, and despite all his impracticalities, he is *dans le vrai*, and the worldly-wise are not. Among the more dedicated and devoted *Cervantistas* this estimate of the book generally prevails; and when one starts to look at the novel from this point of view, a great many of the major incidents do fall into fairly consistent line. The knight is less frequently and less brutally beaten, as the story advances. He finds everywhere sympathy with and from masqueraders, mummers, pastoral pretenders, and dramatic deceivers, who alter for their own purposes the arbitrary values of this world. His own talk grows more and more theological, not to say saintly, till Sancho is driven to comment on it. He finds, again and again, societies where the great of this world humble themselves to the condition of simple folk; and he

creates, climactically, conditions where a simple man of
good heart acquits himself well in a position of worldly
authority.

And yet, about all the accounts which one has read of
Don Quixote as the Divine Simpleton, the religious martyr,
there lingers something artificial and factitious. For though
the knight becomes a religious figure, he never quite ceases
to be a buffoon—a fool and sometimes a brute. He continues to beat and be beaten; he is giggled at by chamber-
maids; he trips while dismounting from Rosinante, claps
a helmet full of curds on his head, and generally makes a
thousand foolish mistakes and ridiculous blunders. There
is nothing divine about most of these blunders, they are
merely a buffoon's stage business; and, in contrast to those
who see the novel as a Christian pilgrimage, there are those
who insist that it never ceased to aim merely at entertain-
ment, on a rather low level of slapstick humor.

The real problem has to do with defining the novel's
texture; for, like the landscape its characters inhabit, *Don
Quixote* itself is alternately strict and flimsy, exemplary
and impudent. One consequence of this circumstance is that
the novel must, inevitably, be very difficult to judge as a
whole. On the more exalted, "religious" level, it is bound
to seem diffuse and almost aimless in many passages. Yet
in just as many other passages the overtones point unmis-
takably to a religious significance which deepens so steadily
as the novel progresses that one cannot possibly suppose
it accidental; indeed, one cannot suppose it other than the
"real" and significant structure of the work. Hence the only
large-scale structure one can see in the book turns out to
be irrelevant, even antagonistic, to major elements within
it. If Don Quixote is really divine or a type of the divine,

we are pained to see him behaving like an ordinary simpleton. If he is a simpleton, our laughter at his antics can only be troubled by the suspicion that he is divine.

In effect, *Don Quixote* thus poses a question to the reader, offers him a dilemma, in a very exact sense *teases* his nerves. Its total impact is not unitary; it does not leave one in a state of repose. Even though Don Quixote is rendered sane at the end of the novel, restored to the arms of mother church and then to the dust from which he came, the novel is still, in the broader sense, unresolved. By every act of delay, every irrelevant excursus, the book has fought against its own conclusion—that unitary view of life which (however great its rewards in terms of this world or the next) gives one no chance to maneuver, to elude, to improvise. There is, then, an odd sort of structural significance to the very violations of "structure" which Cervantes commits; or, to put the matter another way, a view of life as improvisation demands a structure which shall be infinitely open and infinitely extendable.

In the end, human life, however conceived, becomes subject to the ultimate simplification of death. Death puts an end to all fantasies, chimeras, and equivocations. Death is a stripping away of life's many colors by which we come to see God in a cold white light. Don Quixote is given a strict and Catholic death, and one could not, in love and charity, wish it anything else. But what is life? Can one separate its religious core from the enveloping human absurdity, short of the grave? The answer of the novel is, No, for the art by which it has existed, as a novel, is intricately to entangle the two elements—to baffle, and delight, and disappoint, in a word, to tantalize the reader. And one aspect of this art is epitomized in the Moorish scribe Cide Hamete Benengeli, whose manuscript the greater part of *Don Quixote* purports to be.

Cide Hamete is usually discussed as an element in the mingled reality planes with which Cervantes undeniably enjoys playing. This aspect of the novel is too threadbare to merit further analysis; and Cide Hamete serves an evident purpose in it by putting the greater part of the story at a remove from Cervantes, the literal narrator. The old Arabic manuscript may also be considered a device— no more than half serious, to be sure—for evading religious responsibility for the story. Cervantes could scarcely hope to acquire very much immunity from the Inquisition by filtering his fable through an obviously fake Moorish manuscript. But the very existence of Cide Hamete might perhaps be taken as an implicit disavowal and apology. Cervantes' prologue, which disavows so many things that the novel later performs, declares that he has no intention "to preach to anyone, mingling the human with the divine; which is a kind of motley in which no Christian understanding should be dressed." But the Moor may very well don this sort of motley. And, above all, he serves to suggest a world of myth, magic, and imagination, a world subject to its own laws, where the otherwise universal Christian dispensation is, perhaps only for the moment, held in abeyance.

At the risk of imposing on the novel a sort of intellectual ostentation which it has had the wonderful tact to avoid completely, one may recall a strain of thought, existing within the Christian tradition itself, which emphasizes several disparate spheres of human life. For St. Augustine, whose influence on Cervantes is more than a matter of speculation, the spiritual life is both an inevitable consequence of the social life and an inevitable antagonist of it. Peace is, for Augustine, the end and object of both religious and natural life. Peace is the objective of war itself, a necessity of our natures, a necessity even of the most perverse, solitary, and unnatural of men. Yet neither in the house, the city, nor the world is there any complete and unassailable peace; seeking to fulfill the desires of this world, man is drawn to transcend and then to negate them. Social peace is a natural good, to which one must sacrifice many instinctive goods; just so, religious peace is a supernatural good, to which one must sacrifice many social goods.

In this hierarchical scale of values the moral quality of an experience may often be determined more by its relation to the scale than by its own specific nature. In the most extreme form this amounts to nothing more than the observation that behavior which would degrade an angel might well elevate a man. More intimately, what is good in a limited context may be bad in a larger one. The devil himself, who is malice incarnate, must be at peace in many lesser respects in order to pursue his larger war more efficiently. If one sees with divine amplitude the whole range and hierarchy of moral scales and tones, doubt is impossible; the lesser value is subordinate always to the greater, and the culminating value is a peace which transcends even as it negates the experience of this life—the communion of the saints. But in the limited contexts of this world confusions occur; one finds that actions good in themselves serve to advance evil ends and that the most sublime objectives faithfully pursued may lead to social disaster.

The comedy of *Don Quixote*, then, is built upon the trembling relativism generated by an absolute hierarchy of values; its fragility derives from the circumstance that, seen only one stage more deeply or shallowly, any situation will fall into absolute order. To free galley slaves is on the shallow social level an act of simple folly; it is also on the deeper religious level a fulfillment of the command to love one's neighbor as oneself; it is an act of absolute peace. What is funny is to see it as both things at the same time without relating the two visions. The structure of *Don Quixote* is an extended guerilla action against the recognition of unlimited truth. The vision of the author is squint, sidelong, and cockeyed, like a troll's or a necromancer's. Hence, one surmises, Cide Hamete.

In dealing with a book so shimmering, evanescent, and elusive as *Don Quixote*, the commentator is faced with an extraordinary disadvantage. Without doing it a violence, he cannot tie down the book to any set of simple polarities, any elementary antinomy. Yet to say helplessly that the book is shimmering, evanescent, and elusive is to distinguish nothing. I shall not, then, labor the particular sort of equivocation which seems to be represented by Cide Hamete as in any way "explaining" *Don Quixote* or providing any sort of handle by which to grasp this multifarious and many-sided creation. Yet if we think openness of form, ambivalence of judgment, and indefinite equivocation responsible to any degree for the peculiar effect of Cervantes' novel, it may be interesting to see who accepted this valuation of it and why. The "Cervantes tradition" inevitably includes a great many elements, as a book so prismatic and refractory must inevitably be a great many different things to different people; and its "influence" has been traced in a great many different directions on a great many different levels. Novels about rogues and rascals, satires on chivalry, comic epics in prose, plays with shifting reality levels, stories of misguided idealists—all are judged to show the influence of Cervantes, and perhaps do. But from the aspect of the open form two interesting variants are Flaubert and Stendhal, both admirers (and, to some extent, conscious followers) of Cervantes, both deeply engaged in exploiting unresolved attitudes and conflicts but irresistibly different in the total effect they derived from a common technique.

Madame Bovary, as it concentrates on the conflict between the instinctive and the social life, produces an effect which is essentially pathetic. To be sure, the heroine is a creature of some imagination; indeed, she is a more capacious receptacle of experience than anyone else in her miserably pinched and insensitive world. But her imagination is so radically undercut by the satiric overtones with which the author presents it, so trite and sentimental and weak, that it scarcely qualifies as "imagination." In effect, it is something much closer to daydreaming. In her emotions, on the other hand, and in her physical responses, she is immensely rich; and the reader is asked—in at least one passage, specifically asked—to give fuller assent to her emotional impulses than to the imaginative and verbal forms in which they are dressed. Rodolphe is described as bored by Emma's adoring phrases:

He had so often heard these things said that they did not strike him as original. Emma was like all his mistresses; and the charm of novelty, gradually falling away like a garment, laid bare the eternal monotony of passion, that has always the same forms and the same language. He did not distinguish, this man of so much experience, the difference of sentiment beneath the sameness of expression. Because lips libertine and venal had mur-

mured such words to him, he believed but little in the candor
of hers; he thought that exaggerated speeches hiding mediocre
affections must be discounted;—as if the fulness of the soul did
not sometimes overflow in the emptiest metaphors, since no
one can ever give the exact measure of his needs, nor of his con-
ceptions, nor of his sorrows; and since human speech is like a
cracked tin kettle on which we hammer out tunes to make bears
dance when we long to move the stars [II, xii].

Passion is eternally monotonous, yet it is Rodolphe's blindness that he does not distinguish differences of sentiment
beneath sameness of expression; there is a suggestion of
impasse here, but it is resolved by the fluent, murmuring
pathos of the last sentence into an assertion of the truth
(and variety) of sense and sentiment even when buried
beneath sameness of language and convention. This assertion of Emma's rich and essentially unspoiled sensuality is
consistent, too, with other parts of the novel. Her life as
a girl is both remembered and portrayed as rich in natural
pleasures; in his song the blind beggar hideously parodies
her dreams of emotional and sensual fulfillment; and it is
in terms of the five senses that Flaubert phrases his final
deathbed benediction of Emma. Essentially, Emma opposes only wretched animal desire to the inadequate forms
available to her imagination, the miserable self-satisfac-
tions of Homais' Franklinism, the routine palliatives of
religion, and the exquisite torture of being a woman, a
romantic, and a provincial in the nineteenth century.

This major conflict is resolved, almost masochistically,
in the crushing of Emma, in the gruesome details of her
hunting down and desertion and suicide. On this level
the form of the novel is almost too devastatingly closed.
And Flaubert has set the story of Emma within the pro-

logue and epilogue of Charles, partly to gain a perspective on his heroine as bourgeoise, but partly to show society as implacable in its stupidity, as flowing over and around the dead Emma like an irresistible stream of traffic. On the other hand, the crushing of Madame Bovary at the emotional and instinctive level is a consequence of her effort to rise above society as well as to escape its restrictions, to find a kind of love which is at once silly and necessary, which any society is wrong to deny but which no society can possibly provide. The equivocations and irresolutions of this vision are maintained by Flaubert in magnificent, aseptic, attenuated purity throughout the novel.

Emma despises society; society despises Emma; they are both right. Society wants to make her a slave, to reward her with a twenty-five-franc medal for fifty-four years of drudgery; she wants society to be, not like the weekend at Vaubyessard, but like that weekend forever prolonged, freshly seen through eyes eternally innocent. She is a fool in a society of knaves. Her dream is of a world beyond boredom; she is absurd in her expectations of life. But life is absurd in its expectations of her—that she shall admire Charles, respect Homais, and applaud the mutilation of Hippolyte as a triumph of sweetness and light. This impasse is complete.

Emma, then, as has often been observed, is a female Quixote; but she is also a female Sancho, an intruder from the rich, appetitive world of the peasantry. And the blessing is on her appetites, not her fantasies. In fact, the novel contains no center of intellectual attraction powerful enough to set against the assent which is given to Emma Bovary's sensual appetites—her craving for the last drop of liqueur in the glass, the longing which she pours into her love affairs, the luxury and extravagance which are but the superficial forms of her passion for vital experience. Her imagination is a poor, stereotyped faculty, capable of creating only blue landscapes populated by languorous, adoring gentlemen. Her experiences with religion fail to suggest a principle capable of inspiring faith, let alone devotion. She debauches the idea of penitence into a schoolgirl's sentimental orgy, converts the cathedral at Rouen into a boudoir in which she receives her lover, and when she comes to the Abbé Bournisien with a genuine spiritual problem, experiences nothing but humiliation and rebuff. For a moment, indeed, as she escapes from the cathedral with Léon, we are reminded that religion used once to be more than a masquerade. But it is only the beadle, who importunes them, as they flee, to depart by the north porch, "so as to see the Resurrection, the Last Judgment, Paradise, King David, and the Condemned in Hell-flames."

For the rest, if we seek an alternative to the church, we are thrown back on Homais, Charles, and the marvels of modern science; and these, after the butchery performed on Hippolyte, are all but unredeemable. One figure alone appears to enlighten the dismal view of science and all its works. Dr. Larivière does not make his appearance until late in the novel, not, in fact, till the protagonist is already dying; and he says practically nothing. His one significant sentence is a joke on the subject of Homais' intelligence; it is blunt enough, yet perfectly incomprehensible to the bourgeois mind. Its effect is to set Dr. Larivière on another plane than the pharmacist and his colleagues. Strict, severe, unbending, he practices virtues he does not preach or for that matter even believe in; "he would almost have passed for a saint," Flaubert tells us, "if the keenness of his intellect had not caused him to be feared as a demon."

This formidable figure does indeed counterbalance the life of the senses, after a fashion; for the doctor personifies Flaubert's own clinical, analytical intellect, exemplified through the whole novel and here given a local habitation. In this capacity he adds a dimension to the novel; a spare, contemptuous specter, he stalks like a satiric Ibsenite demon the knaves and fools who have been Flaubert's whipping boys. But he is invulnerable, not Quixotic; in contact with the truth that kills (even as it saves), he represents an ultimate, and so he not only appears late in the novel but plays little part in it.

Thus the texture of Flaubert's book represents an odd compound of hard and soft; the essential pathos of Madame Bovary is balanced by the rigid hard-mindedness with which her condition is diagnosed. So far as Charles, Rodolphe, and Léon are concerned, she is bludgeoned throughout with the classic masculine weapon of indifference; but the cruelest weapon used against her (which provokes the reader's most profound sense of horror) is the icy understanding of Dr. Larivière. There is an easy, almost a contemptible way to tell the tale of Emma Bovary; one sees it in a Portuguese variant of the story, *Cousin Bazilio*, by Eça de Queiroz. Here the misbehavior of Luiza with her cousin Bazilio is followed with full sensual sympathy; what Flaubert called the "Paul de Kock" elements in the story are allowed full rein. But Bazilio is made a blackhearted seducer, an incredibly calculating and indifferent Rodolphe; and the consequences of Luiza's misbehavior are brought home to her by a scheming servant girl, Juliana, who blackmails her. Finally discovered by her husband, our heroine succumbs in exemplary fashion of a brain fever. The whole fable thus takes on the quality of a rather gross-minded *exemplum* for young marrieds: "The wages of adultery is brain fever." It is to the infinite credit of Flaubert (and perhaps a consequence of that cool, impersonal, remote perspective which he celebrates in Dr. Larivière and makes use of himself), that no one has ever felt tempted to draw so common a moral from *Madame Bovary*.

By denying Emma all intellectual resource, then, and by opposing to her in his own point of view an outlook so spare, strenuous, and self-defeating as to be practically nihilistic, Flaubert has created the effect of a ruthless pathos, a sentimentality surgically dissected. A streak of masochism runs through the book, revealed by Flaubert's famous identification; its effect is to block out the opposing forces in almost monolithic simplicity. Carried only one short step further, this attitude leads us to the explicit identification of sensitivity, intelligence, and disease, an identification exploited with shattering effect on the purely instinctual level by Tennessee Williams, in *A Streetcar Named Desire*. Like Eça de Queiroz, Williams writes a *Bovary* without a philosophy; but whereas Queiroz substitutes the gross formulas of popular morality, Williams rests in the naked collision of neurosis and society. Society cruelly withholds love from a woman capable of it; seizing at sex as a substitute, she provokes retaliation and is crushed. Blanche is cultured, even intelligent, at least by comparison with Mitch and Stanley; she talks of Poe and Whitman and makes a pretense of refinement. But she is totally lacking in resilience, almost defiantly incapable of practical action against the society which crushes her. Thus there is a heavy, ponderous quality to her fate, which is pathetic and passive in almost unexampled degree. Such a development was implicit, at least partially, in the original Quixote story. The Divine Simpleton, watered down to the Good Simpleton, is defeated not simply by the way of the world but by the way of a particularly wicked and contemptible world. The whole story is transposed down one register, and the effect is therefore pathetic, not to say self-pitying—that is, soft with a touch of hardness, rather than (as in *Don Quixote*) hard with a touch of softness in the perspective.

In a work of this tonality the effect is clearly not tragic, nor is the form closed, even when the action is properly completed; our understanding is directed one way, our sympathy another, and there is no more trace of *catharsis* in the audience than there can be a measurement of *hubris* in the protagonist. A massive identification takes place, but neither release nor transfer; when the character in whom our hopes of struggle and protest have been centered makes her fatal acquiescence, the effect is that of an inner wound, such as the mind feels when a helpless animal falls beneath the slaughter-house hammer. One feels like protesting on behalf of the creature, which, as life, has a perfection of its own; yet one's protest is fatally compromised, not only by the creature's acquiescence, but by one's knowledge that the life itself has been brought into existence only for the purpose of this destruction. And it is the essence of the Quixotic ambivalence, taken at the Flaubert level, that one should explicitly feel the mind of the creator behind that of the character, vindictively dooming its own creation in order to generate in the reader a kind of shocked protest. This protest properly includes neither pity nor terror nor guilt; for each of these emotions has its own relatively self-contained cycle, and the form of the Flaubertian openness is a brutal violation of a being too compromised even to protest. Kafka alone knows something like this effect, for his characters are defeated in their innermost existence, in their estimate of their independent selves, even before society passes its implacable judgment on them.

But there is also a hard, comic, and resilient version of the Quixotic ambivalence, which falls halfway between the line of the satirist and that of the sentimentalist and builds its existence out of their opposition. The Flaubert novel is formed around a wide and sweeping contrast between aggregated masses of social energy: health, fecundity, stupidity, ugliness, and the social norms are piled up on one side; emotional receptivity, imagination, weakness, and beauty are joined on the other. The comic novel, on the other hand, works with narrower moral distances, shorter rhythms, more intricate episodes. Flaubert is all impetus, identification, agglomeration, and the massing of emotional battalions for the spectacular Waterloo of Emma (with Homais playing the Duke of Wellington); Stendhal sticks his Waterloo in the foreground of *The Charterhouse of Parma* in order deliberately to emphasize the smallness of his real theater, and in the theater itself he is constantly reminding us of the narrow bounds which divide the true from the meretricious, the stupid from the inspired, the prudent from the foolhardy. Indeed, his favorite theater is that of the individual ego; he aims, ordinarily, at particularity and distinctness, rather than impetus or agglomeration. From each single fact or idea his prose strikes a line perpendicular to the narrative. And what makes him particularly exciting for a modern reader is the way in which he uses a single set of eyes variously placed, or several sets of eyes, including his own, to draw a whole sunburst of perpendiculars from a single center of concentrated experience. The style is built around an essential tension between the narrative line and the line of direct observation and commentary which deliberately interrupts, punctuates, and angles into it.

The agglomerative Flaubert novel, when it loses just the least edge of its control, degenerates at once into a list; one sees this as a list of stage properties in *Salammbô* and as just a plain sequence of lists in *Bouvard et Pécuchet*. The Stendhal novel is irregular and unpredictable; the story often gives a sense of being told in spite of the author, who, as he passes a given incident, is straining to catch some revelation of character, some hint of a general but apparently irrelevant truth. A kind of arbitrariness lingers about the Stendhal fiction; the author seems to be protesting that he wouldn't possibly want to tell the story as he does if it hadn't just happened so. This gives an air of drama to the most undramatic and antidramatic incidents. For example, Julien Sorel's last tryst with and farewell to Madame de Rênal (*The Red and the Black*, vol. I, ch. xxx) is deliberately made anything but a Wagnerian love scene. All sorts of difficulties supervene, psychological as well as geographical; Julien must campaign for two adventurous hours to arouse his fair enemy's tenderness ("he slipped his hand around the waist of his mistress; this movement was highly dangerous"). He must play his trump card, the departure for Paris, and play it hard, without any assurance of the effect it will produce. In a word, he must transform himself into a frigid politician and his victory into a formal triumph obtained by artifice. And what is gained by this

ruthless sacrifice of the large effect, the sweeping identification? A sense of psychological particularity, in the first
place, an awareness of the complexities of a self-conscious
mind which undertakes to act heroically. The fascination
of this mind is not simply its unpredictability, though it is
constantly and fascinatingly unpredictable; its triumph is
the sense of inner resource which emanates from its behavior. Because Stendhal's unit of narrative is the incident,
his heroes and heroines approach each episode in their
careers freshly and, whatever they learn or fail to learn
from experience in the social sense, never cease to be sur-
prised and enlightened by their own reactions to life. They
are at once actors and audience at the dramas of their own
destinies; and the height of their achievement is to take over
the composition not only of their own characters but of
their own fates from the circumstances in which they have
been cast.

Because of the tragic ritual with which it concludes,
The Red and the Black probably looks more like a novel in
the closed form than *The Charterhouse of Parma*, which
was hastily huddled toward a conclusion for lack of time,
space, and perhaps energy. But the real openness of both
these novels has as little to do with their endings as does that
of *Don Quixote;* they are open, not in the sense that the
ending fails to resolve or terminate the action, but more
elaborately and subtly. One quality of their openness is the
infinite sequence of recessed commentators: the character
comments on himself, the author on his characters; and, by
an odd quality of pseudo-ingenuous surprise, the usual effect
of bustling authorial intervention is transformed, and the
author himself appears amazed at quirks and flairs of temperament which are beyond his invention. More than this

—both the great novels of Stendhal are inconclusive adventures in self-discovery in which only the Protean powers of the ego to shift, vary, twin, invert, and deceive are finally discovered. Whether Julien Sorel is a Jesuit or an anti-Jesuit, a man of ambition or a man of passion, a cold rationalist or a superstitious sentimentalist, a radical or a royalist—all these questions are answered a little ambiguously throughout *The Red and the Black;* and without much effort we can be persuaded to allow the hero something of all these opposed characters. But if we do not really grasp his quality as an individual and coherent soul, much less can we reach any ultimate decision about the two magnificent women who are his destiny. The maternal tenderness of Mme. de Rênal is set against the cold, egotistical passion of Mathilde. Which conforms more naturally to Julien's inner nature? If there is any commentary or resolution, it concerns only the chameleon soul of the hero, who is as adaptable in love as in politics or religion. Thus, to judge Julien we turn to his mistresses, and to judge his mistresses we turn back to Julien; but in truth one of the great meanings of the novel is the mere virtuosity of experience which the hero achieves. At every stage the story verges on the flabbiness and flamboyance of "romantic" rhapsodies like *Corinne;* but the search after experience for its own sake (which, in the absence of inner tension, easily gives rise to watery declamation) is redeemed by an unresolved and perhaps unresolvable doubleness of thought and style. Like his characters, the author is always conscious and critical of himself; his passionate fancies beat continually against the dry energy of a mind which, however limited its stock of ideas, is incurably and untiringly self-conscious.

So it is, too, with Fabrizio del Dongo; like Julien, he is an old-young man, neither quite out of the church nor altogether in it; politically rebellious and at the same time politically conforming, he too is haunted by two loves, one maternal, the other poetic. The novel celebrates comically, sometimes almost farcically, its hero's ability to make the simultaneous best of all these irreconcilable worlds. On what other terms can one understand the cult of hypocrisy which culminates in Clelia Conti's classic evasion of her vow never to see Fabrizio again?

All this suggests that irresolution is, in the fiction of Stendhal, a form of continuing rather than climactic experience; it is not a fatal discovery, but the essential texture of things, a moral climate which the happy few joyously inhale, rather than a poison which dramatically destroys them. Death and finality are found only in the various systems, which simplify life as they limit it and confine one to such single, stupid roles as those of liberal, reactionary, voluptuary, saint, or man of affairs. But if he can preserve himself against these various forms of ossification, the free spirit is subject only to the dooms which he pronounces, for purely arbitrary reasons, on his own spirit.

About these doom judgments there lingers continually the suspicion of arbitrariness and perversity. Julien Sorel willfully condemns himself by his speech to the jury, and the demise of Fabrizio del Dongo is traced, by a series of inconsequential logical "consequences," to the death of a son whom in life he had never regarded with any particular affection. The Stendhal hero is a delicate organism, balanced on the edge of superstition and disdain for the deity; when the terms on which he can have life become a little onerous, he contemptuously chooses his own death. Yet in terms of popular morality he is quite unscrupulous; and the choice of which morality is to govern, in any particular circumstances, always seems to come from an abyss of which we have no knowledge. The openness of the fictional form is a product of Stendhal's openness before the two ethics he espoused; and while this openness has its inevitable stopping point, it has no proper, foreordained conclusion.

Stendhal's well-known prediction, made in various forms, that he would not come into his own till the end of the nineteenth century or the beginning of the twentieth, is verified in this detail of structure, as well as in more obvious particulars. It is not till the twentieth century, and the advent of authors like André Gide and his imitator Aldous Huxley, that one finds openness of form used to something like the effects which Stendhal derived from it: for comic cross-commentary, dramatic highlighting, and expression of an ethical openness before the forms of experience. But, along with the solidity of Stendhal's footing in eighteenth-century rationalism, the boldness of his characterization and the firmness of his narrative line have been dissolved by the skepticisms of later centuries; and his themes, thus transposed, have turned into quite different pieces of music.

From the beginning Gide was enthralled by the possibilities of multiple openness in fiction and devoted to experiments in the form. *Paludes* is deliberately inconclusive in its circularity, moving its nameless hero through six days of aimless half-activity only to return him to exactly the position and turn of dialogue with which he started. It is deliberately unresolved in its "significance," going so far as to ask the reader himself to enlighten the author on his meanings and describing itself in the dedication as "a satire of—what?" By a familiar trick of perspective, it is itself represented within the framework of its own composition; its protagonist is a man who is writing *Paludes*. And finally, its central concern is an escape from types, roles, expectations, and continuities of all sorts. A schedule is made only to be broken, an assertion is made only to be contradicted, the volume itself undertakes to contain its own refutation. Here, indeed, is the whole Gidean world in miniature.

Indecision, egotism, and subtle self-analysis, giving rise to a passion for the divine unforeseen, the unscheduled moment of exact truth—these elements, vividly exemplified in *Paludes*, are the keynotes of Gide's entire career. In all three respects he seems not so much to imitate Stendhal as to press the basic components of the Stendhal mystique further and ever further from resolution and even from stability. The combination of desire and terror which is, for Stendhal, the essence of passionate love, becomes in Gide a total ambivalence, a kind of Manichaeism of the affections. As he vibrated between heterosexual asceticism and homosexual permissiveness, so he prolonged his hesitation between Calvinist conscience and Catholic worldliness, inventing or adapting Dionysian-Apollonian and Hebraic-Hellenistic dichotomies for himself and circling interminably about the natural and acquired ambivalences of his own character. The figures of his fiction tend, for this reason, to fade into an extraordinary thinness; Gide is so intent on their crucial relation to himself and their value as explanations of his own character that he does not give them much thickness of texture in their own right.

Aside from these technical problems, moreover, Gide, by pushing to its limits Stendhal's emphasis on freedom of personality, stood this concept on its head. His problem thus became, not how to achieve freedom or further freedom, but what to do with it once achieved. Gide's response —one cannot say "solution"—to this problem was the much-discussed *acte gratuit*. The gratuitous, the unmotivated, act is, quite simply, an act motivated by the total lack of any motivation; its character becomes quite clear the minute we think of lack of motivation as an active deficiency. Only in an act of meaningless violence rising from the most delicately balanced of opposed appetites and contradictory clarities can the Gidean hero find not resolution but release. Under pressure of outside criticism Gide sometimes asserted that the gratuitous act might perfectly well be philanthropic and benevolent in character, in which case it would normally be called the "disinterested act." He was by nature incapable of making any assertion without an immediate counter-assertion; so in one sense nothing could answer more naturally to the pattern of Gide's ambivalence than this self-correction. But at the same time nothing could answer less naturally to the hard and essentially sinister cast of Gide's mature imagination than a "benevolent" gratuitous act. When he tried to portray one, he fell back immediately upon a hack-Byronic pose and situation which render the magnificent Lafcadio Wliuki quite indistinguishable from Mme. de Staël's Lord Nevile. Rescuing babies from burning buildings is not Lafcadio's proper work at all, and the factitiousness of the incident is apparent.

For a novelist, the problems of casting into narrative form poetico-philosophico-psychologico-dramatic insights like these almost all have to do with thickness of texture and sharpness of outline; and it cannot be said that Gide's solutions to these problems were uniformly triumphant. For an Anglo-Saxon taste, at least, there is something disturbingly diffuse about the fictional forms taken by his thought and feeling. His liking for the journal form, the broken narrative line, and the disjointed moment of insight, combined with the facility of his abstract and many-edged ironies—all these qualities impose sharp limits on the structural effects of which his fictions are capable. Like Joyce, he turned for support to the classic myths and profited, probably more than he was limited, by their stiffness. Still, there is something disturbingly crustacean about this Gidean habit of taking an old shell of fable and filling it with his own veiled, elaborate, allusive ambiguities; it has, often, the air of a great tour de force, till one recognizes that the thought is so subtle and ductile as to be practically amorphous—it could be poured into the mold of almost any myth that happened to be handy. Oedipus, Theseus, Prometheus, Narcissus, Philoctetes, Icarus—each is a slightly different mill to the same Gidean grist.

Yet occasionally Gide was able to get the skeleton of his story where, for a vertebrate audience, it belongs—inside the flesh. In *Les Caves du Vatican* his imagination was at its most Mediterranean, his wit heightened to the fine resilience of humor; and he produced a supremely comic novel of misadventure and cross-purpose. Like the heroes of Stendhal (and like his spiritual kinsman, Bernard, in *The Counterfeiters*), Lafcadio is illegitimate and happy to be so; for bastardy liberates one from all the accumulated traditions of a family. Guided by the artful Protos, whose name (given its own explanation in the purely practical terms of the novel) suggests both Proteus the quick-change artist and the idea of primitive, unformed humanity,

Lafcadio drifts into and out of contact with the usual Gidean band of perverts and pranksters. To him, as to every other major figure in the novel, there comes an abrupt change of life, a complete metamorphosis. From poverty he is raised in a minute to wealth, as Anthime is converted from freemasonry to Catholicism and back again, Amédée sent on a delirious pilgrimage to the Vatican, and Julius driven to renounce his notion of the constantly motivated character. But he is balanced, as the others are not—a self-moved mover.

Lafcadio is a sinister Narcissus, after the fashion of the hero of *Paludes;* balanced, insouciant, and violent, he pursues his own code in relative isolation from the "plots" and is on the verge of slipping out of their orbits entirely, when he carries out the one perverse and pointless action which ends those plots without resolving them. For no particular reason, without even knowing his victim's identity, he pushes Amédée out of a speeding train. Even this action is performed in accordance with a meaningless bit of punctilio. If Lafcadio can count slowly to twelve without seeing a light in the darkened countryside, Fleurissoire may go his way unharmed. At "ten" a light appears, and the execution proceeds.

A man "in love with the unexpected"—this definition of its hero strikes at the heart of the book; and its author has gone out of his way to render the compound of elements as unstable as possible. Although the homosexual themes are pronounced, we leave Lafcadio in bed with Geneviève de Baraglioul; though their attachment is the deepest and most sincere that the book has portrayed, Lafcadio is said already to despise his new mistress a little for her sincerity. Protos, the man of infinite foresight, is made responsible for a murder committed on the spur of the moment; and Lafcadio, though he can easily go scot free, is still tempted, almost compelled, to give himself up. All the while, in the background, the rats which Anthime tortured to illustrate the mechanisms of the conditioned reflex provide ironic commentary on the lowness of those mechanical motivations from which Lafcadio, Julius, and Gide himself are concerned to escape.

Indecision for its own sake—indecision multiplied upon counter-indecision and played against it, till self-consciousness becomes a burden to be laid down through the commission of any violent, meaningless act—this is a central theme of Gide's book. In *Les Caves du Vatican*, a wiry, satiric strength resides in the outlines of the characters, and the game of the false pope is played with such melodramatic zest and absurdity as to give the book an irresistible sparkle. *The Counterfeiters* is a more inward, elaborate, and artful application of the same principles. There is a familiar *trompe-l'oeil* openness in the fact that the novel includes a novelist who is writing a novel precisely on the same subject as *The Counterfeiters;* the very fluidity and complexity which it cultivates are intended to cross and disappoint the single-minded reader. This method is complex, inclusive, and intensely Narcissistic; but even the method is called into question, and its defense resolves itself into a series of infinitely regressed paradoxes about exorcising the devil (who is simply discord and openness as principles in themselves) by evoking him. But because these themes are expounded rather than played with, this book does not have, for one taste at least, the *panache* of its slighter predecessor. Pursuit of the divine unforeseen, evasion of mechanical continuities, and deliberate exploration of contradictory clarities—all these elements carry within themselves the seeds of their own destruction. When the novelist gets self-conscious about his own self-consciousness, the results may be like trying to open the refrigerator door fast enough to see if the light is really off inside. The first and only rule of this fascinating game is not to play it too seriously.

The conflict set up by both Flaubert and Stendhal takes place between a sympathetic-unsympathetic protagonist and a sympathetic-unsympathetic society. Flaubert's mind is undoubtedly more quadrilateral than Stendhal's; when one sees him setting up a sympathy-situation for Emma (her sensual enjoyment of the last drop of liqueur in the glass or her joy in being Leon's pretty mistress), one knows at once that something dreadful (Charles or suicide) is about to happen to her. The effect of inexorability which Flaubert derives from open form is very much like that which we noted in Ibsen's *Ghosts;* the individual is tested against a total impact of meaningless reality and torn apart by it or crushed beneath it. The form is open in this sense, that there is no mediation between individual and society—they are two opposed, irreconcilable, unequal forces, and ultimately they are totally incomparable, like oranges and inevitability. When it has driven Emma to suicide, society has ended the struggle but not resolved it. This is the morbid-ethical horn of the open dilemma, which culminates in overt recognition of a death wish. The self, tested against outer reality, inevitably proves inadequate and so condemns itself; individuality, which is a cancer upon society, can be made such for the individual too, and the only conceivable outcome is suicide.

Stendhal and his fellow travelers represent a comic-aesthetic horn of the same dilemma. Posing the self directly against society and recognizing the inevitability of defeat on these terms, the Stendhal gambit is to conceal and disguise the "real" (i.e., given) self behind masks and self-made myths, to deny continuity, disregard abstract categories, and concentrate on the elaborate observation and perhaps construction of a true self that one hedges on every side with a series of false ones. This too is a sort of test of individuality—personal identity turns out to be the essential problem of open form—but it is a test of the individual's power to exclude, not to include. Intellectually, Stendhal is more perverse than Flaubert; emotionally, quite the contrary. This represents a rough fumbling after the truth that Stendhal's perversity is all on the surface, his manner is close to vaudeville; whereas in Flaubert one senses that the life of feeling has been corrupted at the root. Hence, perhaps, their differing attitude toward verbal art: Stendhal contemptuous of it, Flaubert reverential. So far as Cervantes is concerned, it may be that Stendhal's is the more genuine derivation, both spiritually and artistically; exclusion was Cervantes' problem, too. Yet the sense of perverseness, which we miss almost entirely in Shakespeare and Cervantes, clings even to Stendhal and is heightened disturbingly in Gide; perhaps in poetry, where we are more accustomed to witty ambivalence, a tradition of openness may be discovered in which perversity plays a less persistent role.

~ VI ~

Metaphysical Poets, Ancient and Modern

DONNE AND ELIOT

BY juxtaposing witty contraries and deliberately avoiding the smooth surface of conventional lyricism, the metaphysical poets of the seventeenth century created a kind of structure which is sometimes open and which has proved infinitely adaptable to the moods of the twentieth. Seventeenth-century wit was both serious and funny; this has turned out to accord nicely with various Freudian notions which are dear to our hearts and close to our experience. Colloquial and unflowery speech has fallen gratefully on ears suspicious (for whatever reasons) of facile decoration; and strenuous thought has pleased modern readers, both for its own harsh sake and for the distinction implicit in being able to read it. Eked out with an assist from the French symbolists (with whom they would have been aghast to find themselves coupled), the metaphysicals have become a root influence on modern poetry.

Historically there was no such thing as a "metaphysical school," and a poet-by-poet listing of them is still apt to shade off into some highly ambiguous figures. Certain poems by Ben Jonson are far more "metaphysical" in their thought and feeling than the greater part of Herbert or Marvell. Suckling, Lovelace, Waller, and Samuel Butler are not often thought of as belonging to the "school of Donne"; yet Professor Grierson included them in his important little anthology *Metaphysical Lyrics and Poems of the Seventeenth Century*. The very word "metaphysical," meaningless, in the first place, as only a term derived from library science could be, was not applied to English poets till many years after the best and most famous of them were dead. And the word "school" cannot well describe a casual concatenation of men, largely unacquainted with one another, who happened over a period of fifty or sixty years to write some poems in more or less similar styles.

Although it has been variously, earnestly, and sometimes foolishly described in terms of a peculiar subject matter, metaphysical poetry is best distinguished simply as poetry which makes use of a certain sort of wit. What this variety of wit actually is may well detain us for a moment. It is not distinctively learned wit; for though all the metaphysicals were learned men, Herbert, Marvell, Cowley, and Vaughan, for example, often do not write in a learned style, Donne sometimes does not—and learning is nothing distinctive, for Milton and Shelley were learned poets. Metaphysical wit need not be "serious" for "The Flea," "The Bait," and "The Blossom" are deliberately and thoroughly comical poems. Metaphysical wit need not cultivate occult wisdom, alchemical imagery, and macro-microcosmic correspondences—though traditionally metaphysical poets did prefer this sort of machinery to the Cupids, arrows, torches, and bleeding hearts of Hellenistic amorism. I think, though, that we come a good deal closer to metaphysical wit when we define it as wit based upon a difficult metaphor, intellectual or abstract in its nexus, rather than naturalistic, involving more often an esoteric analogy than a superficial, single-level physical resemblance, and giving always the sense of a difficulty overcome.

Probably the metaphysical style had its origin in the concept of an analogical universe; but this is an historical consideration, not a critical definition. At all events, its most distinctive effect was in making metaphysical poetry characteristically a poetry of stress and strain. For not only were concepts of the analogical universe under sharp challenge during the seventeenth century from competing images of the cosmos, notably the Calvinist and the Copernican, but they were, in and of themselves, subject to a sense of strain, for their lines of harmony are those of an unfallen world. Modern sentimentalists eulogize the days before the great Puritan revolution as a period of unified sensibility; had they lived in the seventeenth century, they would certainly have put the golden age much earlier; and, in fact, only in the Garden of Eden during the twenty-four hours between Creation and Fall did the world actually exist according to the diagrams set forth in E. M. W. Tillyard's *Elizabethan World Picture*.

Thus the analogical universe, which is implicitly a description of the universe as it ought to be, not as it is, was the origin of the metaphysical style; and that style was born with a built-in sense of strain. "Wit," which in its early meanings is not often far removed from general intellectual energy, was conceived of as doing its best to hold this elaborate structure together, extending it through unexpected and daring lines of thought or reinforcing it in

surprising ways by noting unfamiliar correlations between
familiar things. In a poet like Donne, anxious by circumstance and temperament and never without a flavoring of
egotistical showmanship, this attitude came presently to
verge on the view that the juxtaposition of farfetched
similarities in the teeth of superficial disparities was poet-
ically effective in itself.

Dr. Johnson, speaking from the vantage of a simple and
relatively solid aesthetic, found a desire for personal display
at the root of the metaphysical style. His estimate that the
poets were trying to show off their learning was perhaps
too limited; but a desire to display the poet's wit merged
insensibly with a desire to read deeply in the book of creatures, and might often be indistinguishable from it. This
sometimes led to a sinewy, free-wheeling intellectualism
which allowed the poet to follow any argument to its conclusion or even, occasionally, two arguments at once.
Donne is particularly fascinated by the notion of arguments running both ways. Many poets have written of
love in both sexual and spiritual terms; the usual pattern is
either to keep these assertions separate or to subordinate
the fleshly to the spiritual. Donne, in "The Ecstasy," rather
inconclusively reverses the process; starting on the lofty
spiritual level, he feels the need to descend

> T'affections, and to faculties,
> Which sense may reach and apprehend,
> Else a great Prince in prison lies.

Thus love is an inconclusive and unconcluded cycle; rising
from bodies to souls and descending to bodies again, the
lovers go their self-generated way, and an outsider, over-
hearing their "dialogue of one," would see little difference

between the various stages of their commerce. Thus the poem deprecates itself by describing its own action as without beginning or end or importance. Even more striking is "The Funeral," which twists and shifts in several directions at once, being now addressed to mortuary agents who enshroud and bury the poet, now to his mistress; and the attitude toward the mistress is now beseeching, now defiant and mocking. Like "The Blossom," the poem starts as a plea and ends on a defiant note of separation. This sort of irresolution often amounts to something like a structural principle in Donne; having begun a poem in one key, he feels obliged to modulate into another, whether it be up or down, toward or away from a conclusive attitude. Hence many of his poems seem like fragments snipped more or less at random from a longer and more consecutive argument, often beginning and sometimes ending in highly inconvenient places.

Donne's poetry is often irresolute or logically inconclusive; even more potent in contributing to its peculiar quality is the persistent use of metaphors which override without quite suppressing their difficulties. Here we need not go beyond the most famous image of the whole "school," the comparison of separated lovers to the legs of a compass, at the conclusion of "A Valediction Forbidding Mourning":

> If they be two, they are two so
> As stiffe twin compasses are two,
> Thy soule the fixt foot, makes no show
> To move, but doth, if the' other doe.
>
> And though it in the center sit,
> Yet when the other far doth rome,

> It leanes, and hearkens after it,
> And grows erect, as that comes home.
>
> Such wilt thou be to mee, who must
> Like th'other foot, obliquely runne;
> Thy firmnes makes my circle just,
> And makes me end, where I begunne.

The incongruities in this image are latent but nonetheless potent; for most of us, plane geometry does not have much to do with the feelings engendered by leaving a mistress. Indeed, there is no denying that these feelings find somewhat attenuated expression through the ingenuities of the image; grief which has leisure to work out the details of such extravagant metaphors is not, in any but the literary sense, "serious." The metaphor all but blocks out the subject which it is ostensibly invoked to illuminate. It offers a resistance; and to the degree that it does so Donne undeniably intended to give an impression of himself as the mind in which such a simile took shape.

To say this is not to deny directly that Donne's image is decorous. Of course it is in several ways, some of them completely novel to English literature. It is not in the least decorous to the topic if this is a witty image, as the world for three hundred years has taken it to be; for decorum, whatever else it is, will not be substantially identified with wit until the eighteenth century. But the image is decorous to the way in which a certain mind may be imagined as viewing the subject; it is decorous in relation to the actor. Thinking of a mistress who is distant physically but united to him by bonds of thought and affection, Donne is not repelled by but rather welcomes the idea of gaunt, stalking, exact compasses. He is not precisely saying, "Look what a

curious fellow I am to be making this odd connection";
still, if there is any focus to the image at all it is on the mind
that conceived and is to be imagined speaking it. In short,
Donne is operating here very much after the manner of
what a later age will call the dramatic monologue. One
striking characteristic of this style is the degree to which it
depends on the reader for its own completion. By providing raw materials out of which the reader is invited to
construct a personality, the poem achieves indirectness,
indefiniteness of meaning, and boldness of contour, which
are very attractive poetic commodities.

It has been something of a fashion to look down one's
nose at Donne's self-consciousness, to suggest "the shadow
of an impure motive" in his writing, the possibility of "a
facile success." He is often theatrical, not simply in his
love poetry, where since Petrarch we have grown more or
less inured to masks and disguises, but in the sacred sonnets,
like "Batter my heart," or "Spit in my face, you Jews."
But Donne's "impurity" is not simply personal; it is a
quality common to most metaphysical poets, Herbert and
Marvell no less than Donne. They are dramatic poets who
play with a contrast between spheres of existence: the
microcosm and the macrocosm or the stadium of heavenly
simplicity and that of worldly complexity or the sphere of
contemplation and the sphere of action. Their style is metaphysical precisely as it juxtaposes points of view which are
in some ways compatible, in other ways not—as it carries
out a juxtaposition which involves a strain. Dryden finds
that Donne and his followers "affected the metaphysics"
by including abstract speculation in love poems "where
nature only should reign"; Eliot says they affected undue
popularity, via a sort of exhibitionism which left "nature"

too much play altogether. But if metaphysical poems operate, by definition, in at least two spheres, their proceedings
are bound to appear affected to anyone who assumes a
single point of view. A metaphysical poem is one which
makes dramatic use of contrasted points of view; and this
dramatic quality is of the essence. It is plain, for example,
that God would be bound to find metaphysical poetry completely meaningless. His nature being metaphysical per se,
and reconciling all contradictions beforehand, He could
not possibly see any point in the strained ingenuity of
metaphysical contrast-metaphors.

It by no means implies a derogation of his immense poetic
achievement to point out that Eliot himself has been particularly skillful in his manipulation of dramatic contrasts.
As early as "The Love Song of J. Alfred Prufrock" one
notes the shrewd application of "difficult" metaphors, that
is, metaphors which operate on the attraction-repulsion
principle of the compass image, to illustrate a dramatic
character.

> Let us go then, you and I,
> Where the evening is spread out against the sky
> Like a patient etherized upon a table.

Dissection is the central theme of "Prufrock"; the poem is
in essence a major operation performed upon himself by a
reluctant surgeon; yet we know none of this beforehand,
and the invitation to a quiet evening stroll is strikingly and
deliberately incongruous with this image of the operating
table. The incongruity is emphasized by a major shift in
rhythm, a break in rhyme, an abrupt twist of feeling. "Prufrock" being explicitly a dramatic monologue, one may
urge that the discontinuity, hesitation, and repetition of the

protagonist's thoughts imitate the actual working of a reluctantly self-dissecting mind and hence are devices of unity. On another level, however, the author's dependence on the reader to complete and unify the fragments of which the poem consists makes the openness of his verbal pattern apparent.

> I should have been a pair of ragged claws
> Scuttling across the floors of silent seas.

There are perhaps a half-dozen facets of Prufrock's character which relate directly to this image; [1] but the character is itself a hypothesis of the reader's, and the effect of the image is to become decorous by helping to create the thing to which it is decorous.

There is no point in dwelling at length on the large structural opennesses of Eliot. *The Waste Land* has been nicely described as a novel with all the story left out, and it is a familiar point that the social circumstances opened up by this modern epyllion are most sketchily countered by the incantation *Datta, Dayadhvam, Damyata;* indeed, it has been urged by the unregenerate that putting these improving injunctions in Sanscrit was Eliot's only recourse against the helpless laughter to be anticipated from a bald assertion. Since then it has been apparent that resolution, where it occurs in Eliot's plays and poems, is achieved

---

[1] He is a submerged personality, prudish and also rock-proof against sexual involvement, hence incapable of frolicking in the fresh air with mermaids, furtive and crablike because his mind proceeds sidewise, disgusting because invertebrate, hardshelled because committed to a grotesque and rigid social role, a floor crawler like the insects pinned and wriggling on the wall, and ragged because torn by his own thoughts as by a case of knives. There is not much to Grover Smith's suggestion of an echo from *Hamlet* II, 2, 204–206, except that Hamlet mentions a crab.

largely by exclusion. The great effects of *Four Quartets* are built largely on a resolute sinking out of the middle world of here and now down into the self and subself, or else up into the sphere of unchanging universals and abstractions (the way up and the way down being here very strikingly one and the same). Where the everyday world could not be left altogether behind, as in the plays, it was granted, not without a touch of condescension, a place of its own. There are two ways, in *Murder in the Cathedral* almost as distinctly as in *The Cocktail Party;* both plays are about the differences in those ways and, in a sense, about the choice between them. But ultimately there is no choice in either play; for the decision between the ways turns out to be merely an expression of one's nature, nature being taken in a sense which is beyond choice.

Long ago, Paul Elmer More remarked a distinction of tone, feeling, and intellectual content between Eliot's prose, which seemed "classical," and his verse, which could only be described as "romantic." Eliot himself remarked, by way of helping things out, that his poetry dealt with things as they are (fragmentation, degeneracy, multiplicity) and his prose with things as they ought to be (order, hierarchy, and Anglo-Catholicism). But this was long ago; a contemporary writer on Eliot would have to draw two lines, one horizontal through the poetry just after *The Waste Land,* the other vertical through all the plays so far. If not a conflict, this is a major difference; it is the difference in temper and attitude between "Prufrock" and *The Idea of a Christian Society,* between *The Waste Land* with its outward and *Four Quartets* with their inward vision. Hardening as it becomes more conscious, one finds the division recurring in *The Cocktail Party* as that between the truth

of the Chamberlaynes and the truth of Celia. We are beyond any thought of a *rapprochement* here; the conspira-
torial slyboots who have been initiated into the real truth
about life happily quote Shelley on the double existence
envisaged by the magus Zoroaster; and if it were not too
pretentious, one might be tempted to say that the duel in
Eliot's mind between orthodoxy and cosmopolitanism has
culminated in the creed of the Manichees. That subtle,
clinging, attractive doctrine, which gave so much trouble
to St. Augustine, might fittingly triumph over Eliot and
set a seal on one sort of structural openness in his work.

But this is only the crudest and most speculative of possibilities, for Eliot, to a far greater extent even than Donne,
fights clear of the literal and unequivocal assertion in his
poetry. He is particularly impregnable because he has
added, from the French nineteenth-century symbolists, the
armor of the dandy. Thus his poetry maintains, behind a
polished surface, an enigmatic, uncommitted, unpredictable
stance; it is at once poker-faced and provocative and can
draw freely on the meaningless or unmotivated assertion or
(with diabolical skill) on the revelation that serves only to
distract and conceal. The footnotes to *The Waste Land*
are classic examples of this maneuver; but within the poem
itself there are uses for the symbol that is invoked with an
air of authority and an absolutely uncontrolled range of
associations. A crowd crossed London Bridge, says Eliot,
and

> Flowed up the hill and down King William Street,
> To where Saint Mary Woolnoth kept the hours
> With a dead sound on the final stroke of nine.

The fact is a fact; we have a solemn but not insignificant
footnote to the effect that Mr. Eliot has often observed

the phenomenon which he describes. There is a dramatic note of finality in the line; it is appropriate to have a "dead" sound in a London populated by dead people; the church may prefigure the Chapel Perilous; and the dead stroke certainly prefigures the "reminiscent bells, that kept the hours" of line 283. These are connections within the poem, and we may make further connections with literary "sources" and a physical phenomenon outside the poem; what more do we want? Only this; that as the crowd is an allegorical crowd, borrowed from Dante, we expect to find some allegorical meaning in any motion they take or cease to take, and we are blankly, flatly disappointed. Thus deliberate meaninglessness, or a deliberate shift of meaning levels, is used to give impact to Eliot's poem. We shall see other aspects of this device in a discussion of open form as a device for coping with the irrational.[2]

Meanwhile, it seems clear that Eliot and Donne are key figures in a comparison of ancient with modern metaphysical writers. The division of their work into sacred and profane aspects supports the parallel; the dramatic impurities of temperament which they share, a common nostalgia for discipline, and a similar talent for melodic dissonance, all enhance the pairing. Their minds work in terms of analogy, metaphor, and sympathy under the impulse of a splendid ambition to inclusiveness. Both enjoy the bristle of learning, as opposed to poets like Marvell and Housman, who conceal it under a smooth surface or avoid it altogether. They are not to be tagged as believers in "religion" or "science" *tout court;* Merritt Hughes, in demonstrating that Donne was not a religious skeptic, very effectively shows that he was not a henchman of the new

[2] See ch. viii, below.

philosophy.[3] But then he would not have very much to tell modern readers if he were an earnest Baconian like Cowley; it is precisely because he used the materials of the new and old sciences without committing himself to "belief" in them that he reminds the modern reader of Eliot's dalliance with Frazer, Miss Weston, and those Jungian comparative-religionists who give to Eliot's orthodoxy such a distinct flavor of eclectic generosity.

As for Donne, when one has decided that he was just playing with the new science, there is a natural tendency to think that his devotion to Mistress Religion is somehow made more real, more solid. But this is not necessarily so; because a man doubts Peter, he does not necessarily trust Paul—he may trust a third party or no one. Donne was fascinated by the machinery of theology; he reveled in the possibilities of a metaphysical God, a metaphorical universe, a structure of analogies and types. These beliefs, and the attitudes they involved, served a temperamental and artistic as well as an intellectual or spiritual need. But in the sparse, austere atmosphere of the dogmatic theologian, or even of the fully dedicated contemplative, Donne seems always to have been ill at ease. No doubt it is too much to describe him as just playing with the properties of religion in the way he played with the properties of physical science; still, he can fumble the definitions of faith and contemplation (in Sermon XXIII) as he would never have fumbled a definition of matter. That is, he can be wrong, technically, according to the best thought of the day, about a prime point of that art which he, admittedly, took with the greatest seriousness. It is an old

[3] "Kidnapping Donne," *California Essays in Criticism*, 2d ser. (Berkeley, Calif., 1933).

commonplace that the literary mind may use and even believe in religion or science on many possible levels and without fully understanding either discipline as a discipline.

His own time took little notice of the science-religion conflict in Donne; thirty years after his death that conflict could still be kept peripheral and secondary in the minds of men as conscious as Glanville and Sprat. So far as the age sensed a contradiction in Donne, it was between Apollo's flamen and the true God's priest. And when his contemporaries estimated his achievement in reconciling these two functions, they chose terms which cannot be understood except as describing an exhibition of purely individual strength and energy. It was his "imperious wit" that Carew remembered, the "holy Rapes" that he committed on men's wills; it was the character of an intellectual tyrant that he attributed to Donne:

> Here lies a King, that rul'd as hee thought fit
> The universall Monarchy of wit.

The parallel with Eliot is obscured a bit here by the terminology of humility which the later poet has affected. Eliot's distrust of ego and self-assertion, his rather formidable restraints and inhibitions, half encourage one to think of him as a classic metaphysical in opposition to Donne, a romantic. There is certainly in Eliot a greater hesitation about personal assertion than one finds in Donne; the perpendicular pronoun is less frequent and more dramatic in its use, further removed from the poet's historical self. The poet has a fondness for speaking from behind masks which reminds us that Robert Browning, as an early and strenuous admiration of Pound's, may well have left his mark on Eliot's first manner. But behind these superficial differences there seems to be an element of positive similarity; Eliot's humility is not at the opposite pole from the sublime and sometimes flashy egotism of Donne, it is (like some other opposites) the same thing, masked. Temperament asserts itself shamefacedly in Eliot because he is aware of its many and varied abuses at the hands of Shelley and Swinburne, Ella Wheeler Wilcox, Whitman, and the Dadaists. But temperament is the only rule of a cosmopolitan culture; even in demanding a discipline which shall repress the extravagances of temperament, one may merely express the deepest of them. "Simple simplicity" is not merely a charming tautology, it is one of the rarest and most fragile of human traits. The trouble is that in a community which does not recognize either their presence or their absence the theological virtues are particularly hard to pursue for themselves. Writers especially, who are committed by their discipline to making a human impression on human beings, seem irresistibly impelled to pursue virtue first and then explain afterward what they have been doing. "See, see! I have been humble!" The arch-hero of this device is of course M. Tartufe; but there are contemporaries too who have put forward a greater flow of language about a vow of silence than would have sufficed for thirty years of normal conversation.

At all events, a basic psychological element in the metaphysical style of Eliot, as of Donne, seems to be the assertion of temperament armed with wit and learning over logical or conventional categories; and this assertion cannot help involving a poet in self-dramatization. When *The Waste Land* mingles quotations from Dante, Webster, Baudelaire, and St. Augustine, they serve to illuminate an ostensible dramatic situation but also, more vividly, to illustrate the mind in which that situation has taken form. If the situation alone were central, the quotations would be distracting; it is their success in casting light two ways at once (thus creating an interplay between personality and situation) that makes them so complex and revelatory. Within the dramatic situation Eliot tends to play a more feminine role than Donne; but, though he withdraws and conceals instead of domineering, he is nonetheless certain to be found at the center of his own stage with all the strings firmly in his hands. As they are metaphysical, his poems are open in their texture from the beginning, and in their larger intellectual structure they have become increasingly so toward the end of Eliot's career. But in the figure of the poet as dandy, a figure who never explains or rationalizes, who dominates his deliberate irrationalities by cultivating a superb poise from which he can disdain to notice them, the old master controls all disparities. Outside the field of judo there is probably no such striking example of the defense which is also an attack, the yielding which is also a controlling, the strength which consists of giving way.

AUDEN AND HERBERT

If metaphysical poetry abandons the flowers of classical rhetoric to cultivate the strong metaphorical line and the direct, colloquial expression, it is ostensibly to concentrate on intellectual tension and the subtleties of metaphor. Yet athletic metaphysical verse does not always triumph without opposition—does not, in fact, always triumph. Instead of deepening the contrast between artistic and ethical truth without resolving it, the metaphysical poet may undertake to solve it, at the expense of the poem itself. The most compressed statements of this impasse, as it struck the seventeenth century, are the poems of George Herbert.

Herbert's chronology is so radically foreshortened and poorly documented that one always runs major risks in assuming any given order of composition among his poems. Still, one obvious arrangement of a few of them seems to bear certain sanctions on the face of it. There are poems of plain dramatic import and rather complex theatrical design, charged with strong metaphors and conflicts of sentiment; an example is "The Collar." Then there are poems, themselves complex in character, which protest the author's desire for simplicity of style, for example, the two poems titled "Jordan." And, finally, there are poems in which the simple style of pure and unadorned statement prevails throughout. Surely it is no radical hazard to see here a developing intention.

At their most light-hearted ("Jordan II"), the poems which plead for simplicity have all the coy artfulness of an old love tradition, by which the sighing amorist elaborately protests that he will use no art.

> When first my lines of heav'nly joyes made mention,
> Such was their lustre, they did so excell,
> That I sought out quaint words, and trim invention;
> My thoughts began to burnish, sprout, and swell,
> Curling with metaphors a plain intention,
> Decking the sense, as if it were to sell.

One is reminded here of Sidney's sonnet against verbal art (see above pp. 4–6). Phrase is piled on phrase, artifice on artificiality, so that the voice of sincere feeling, when it speaks, may express perfect simplicity and directness.

But in "Jordan I" the onslaught against art is sharper, and aimed not at embroidery only but at all verbal fiction:

Who sayes that fictions onely and false hair
Become a verse? Is there in truth no beautie?
Is all good structure in a winding stair?
May no lines passe, except they do their dutie
Not to a true, but painted chair?

This attack on verbal art is particularly interesting because Herbert is so deliberate and inventive in his devices of poetic artfulness. For example, he is given to pruning his rhymes, as in "Paradise"; writing echo poems, as in "Heaven"; shaping his verses into wings and altars, as in "Easter Wings" and "The Altar"; numbering his syllables and using identical rhyme words in consecutive stanzas, as in "Aaron"; weaving his lines into rounds and posies, as in "Sin's Round"; splitting his thoughts, as in "The Watercourse"; or writing deliberate discords in order to resolve them in the last stanza, as in "Denial." These are devices of complexity and art too random to be called "experiments" and too unstrained to be thought of as efforts at "expression." Paradoxically, their real character is that of devices of simplicity; for they try to give the poems a quality of simply existing, of acting independently of what they say. "The Altar" is explicit about this effect:

A   *Heart*   alone
Is   such   a   stone,
As   nothing   but
Thy pow'r doth cut.
Wherefore each part
Of my hard heart
Meets in this frame,
To praise thy Name:
That, if I chance to hold my peace,
These stones to praise thee may not cease.

In a sense, the finest achievement of his poetry is to obliterate its own "metaphysical" quality, to become artless in such a consummate sense that all barriers between the thing as idea and the idea as thing seem to disappear.

The physical existence of his poems as objects was intimate to Herbert; the physical actions they implied were always in his mind; and his finest verse manages to infuse simple physical behavior with a kind of luminous grace from which all sense of effort and strain has completely disappeared.

> Love bade me welcome: yet my soul drew back,
>   Guiltie of dust and sinne.
> But quick-ey'd Love, observing me grow slack
>   From my first entrance in,
> Drew nearer to me, sweetly questioning,
>   If I lack'd anything.
>
> A guest, I answer'd, worthy to be here:
>   Love said, You shall be he.
> I, the unkinde, ungratefull? Ah my deare,
>   I cannot look on thee.
> Love took my hand, and smiling did reply,
>   Who made the eyes but I?
>
> Truth Lord, but I have marr'd them: let my shame
>   Go where it doth deserve.
> And know you not, says Love, who bore the blame?
>   My deare, then I will serve.
> You must sit down, sayes Love, and taste my meat:
>   So I did sit and eat.

The communion represented so flatly and naïvely in these monosyllabic verses is overwhelming in its import; but there is no violence in the expression of it, and the dialogue becomes ever plainer as the poem approaches its climax. Even the wry metaphors and turns of language which mark the first stanza disappear from the third one; only the perfect humility of the images and language, as they play against the majesty of the theme, seem to entitle the poem to the adjective "metaphysical." It is, in fact, a classic example of a metaphysical poem so close to metaphysical reality that it needs no impurities of style, no dramatization or assertion of self; yet its very comportment, its quiet and easy grace, are dramatically eloquent. Parodic denigration of the poem by the poem is a paltry theatrical device alongside the steadily deepening quiet and humility of "Love"; yet even in this exquisite poem there is a carefully calculated anti-poetic element, which culminates in the flat, monosyllabic simplicity of the last lines. Embarrassment and deference are put off, with poetry itself, as the poem ends; the supreme giving is found to be but the humblest and simplest form of taking, and finality can go no further. The form of the lyric is perfectly closed by this action, the form of *The Temple* is closed; so distinct is the sense of the poem's thought transcending poetry itself that "Love" has never been given, among Herbert's poetry, any position but last.

Modern poetry, above all modern poetry which has been touched by the metaphysical manner, knows little of the quiet style; at least if repose is to be had, it is not found in devotion. Our devotional verse is, characteristically, strenuous and difficult; even *Four Quartets* gives the impression of a long ladder to be climbed, up or down, before one reaches not a final vision but the condition of readiness to see a vision which may or may not oblige by appearing. And perhaps the outstanding impression given by modern virtuosi of metaphysical verse like Auden and Empson is of almost incurable restlessness. Insatiably witty, endlessly complex and allusive, their verse is without repose or hope of repose; its twisting and sinuous activity is its own excuse for being, and a casual phrase in this context can only give the impression of pointed, deliberate purpose. The naturalness which for Herbert is something like a sacrament is for Auden and Empson simply one more piece of "busy-ness," a negative to be set among all the positive emphases.

Fragments and distraction—to characterize in these terms the work of the two most eminent and intelligent contemporary practitioners of metaphysical verse is absurdly condescending, for it suggests the easy availability of a unity which they have wantonly declined. Yet the fact is a fact, and needs some critical explaining, that the typical poem by Auden or Empson is verbally busy and yet seems at the end to have moved the reader through so slight an orbit. Auden's "Horae Canonicae," from *The Shield of Achilles*, provide an interesting recent example of these qualities in a context which is ostensibly devotional in nature. The seven poems forming this cycle describe the actions of a mind in the course of a day which is at once any day anywhere, a particular day in a reasonably consistent small town (evidently Mediterranean), and Crucifixion Day, i.e., Good Friday. That the hours are canonical suggests a stronger devotional and ecclesiastical tone than the first six poems actually have. The setting is not, for example, specifically monastic; until we come to "Lauds," which is out of place as the last poem, representing (presumably) the beginning of the next day's cycle, there is not even a clear suggestion of the penitential and ritualistic function of the canonical hours.

Close analysis of the patterns of imagery also yields a somewhat scattered effect. "Prime," for example, describes the poet's awakening as a quelling of the nocturnal rummage of a rebellious fronde, then as an arrival on earth of Adam sinless, guiltless of any act; and finally as a losing of Paradise. It is hard to see here a developing intention; the first view has its truth, and, in terms of the poet's dramatic personality, more truth than the later notions (his "we" is the "we" of a chorus, conservative, social, more aware than daring; there is no "I"). The total effect is of three unrelated, ingenious metaphors for waking up. The poet is anxious that we be aware that he is aware of the Freudian view of dreams; he disarms us by putting it first. But even if we were ultimately supposed to think his dreams Paradisal, there is no actual basis for doing so. Our own dreams, as we have known very well since 1900, are not Paradisal at all; if we are to reverse the established concept, some extra emphasis will be needed, and there is no way of pretending that dream-as-Paradise is not a reversal.

Thus I think the poet is, throughout the "Horae Canonicae," playing with perspective for its own sake. The Crucifixion story itself is toned down to nothing more than a muted emphasis in a mind largely preoccupied with other things: its guilt, its social comforts, its pleasure in half-significant puns ("holy," "wholly"), off-rhymes, and internal rhymes, its self-consciousness. That the speaker cannot recall what happened between twelve and three of his particular Good Friday is, evidently, of the deepest significance; in effect, it is a piece of Freudian business that refers back to, and makes one think of, the rummage of a rebellious fronde, rather than the regeneration of mankind. One point of the poem is, undoubtedly, that mankind finds it painful and ungrateful to be regenerated; but even this point is not made with enough energy to seem more than a by-product of the poem. The poet works so hard to avoid the prophetic and emphatic, he is so versatile and busy in his command of verbal devices and so generous about seeing half-significance for them, that all sense of over-all structure is lost in the murmur and mutter of many muted, restless particulars. The decision to seek this effect was evidently deliberate and is only to be condemned as it makes the poet's own hand (as distinct from his dramatic theme) seem languid, diffuse, and pathetic. There is certainly an over-all shape to the "Horae Canonicae" as a sequence, but it is the arbitrary shape of seven liturgical observations stuffed with a rubble of random thoughts. With a little cleverness almost anything can be fitted into this form, and the form itself, having nothing to struggle against, takes on the aspect of a sack rather than an architecture.

Empson is even more restless as a poet than Auden; but his poetry is so frankly a series of puzzles that it comes under rather a different heading. It does not stalk about its subject making disjointed remarks but operates under higher tension and with a stricter regard for the object— the object being, more often than not, withheld. This is the mode of the literary puzzle; its effect comes from an "open" disparity between the original obscurity of the metaphors used to describe an unknown object and their ultimate appropriateness. But as this smacks of a mechanical contraption manipulated for its own sake, it verges on the variety of trick which this study has arbitrarily excluded from consideration.

Whether dramatic or philosophic, restlessness and strenuosity seem to be closely associated with the metaphysical style. Herbert's repose is a rare thing, achieved by forcing the metaphysical style almost beyond its limits as a style; one might call this achievement visionary metaphysical writing, move down a stage to the philosophic, descend another stage to the dramatic, and reserve a space at the foot of the landing for the mere joke or puzzle, which could be called manneristic. On such a scale, there might be room for still another variety of metaphysical writing, intermediate between the dramatists and the mannerists, where some curious problems of literary taste, both good and bad, are opened up.

CRASHAW AND DYLAN THOMAS: DEVOTIONAL ATHLETES

Because the metaphysical style is not only tolerant of discord but often committed to it as a first principle, critics have frequently asserted that the style invites one kind or another of bad taste. As we have seen, Dr. Johnson thought the radical image was nothing more than an occasion for irrelevant display of the poet's learning or ingenuity. His famous account of the metaphysical poets, in the *Life of Cowley*, points up the faults of the style as exemplified in frigid conceits by Cowley and Cleveland and in some mortuary poems by Donne which it would be hard for any sensitive reader to consider fortunate. But Johnson's blame also falls unerringly on the one image of Donne's which has been most generally taken as a touchstone of the metaphysical manner. Speaking of that famous compass image which we have already discussed, Johnson can say only that he does not know whether ingenuity or absurdity predominates. If this is right, the whole metaphysical style may be subject to the impeachment of bad taste; if, on the other hand, we endorse the compass image, we may be left with only the haziest ideas of taste and bad taste in poetry. The image *is* incongruous; it would not have been discussed so much if it were not. How to defend it without defending other images, which are, or appear to be, indefensible?

The easier line of defense is based upon dramatic or temperamental congruity. The possessor of a gymnastic mind likes to display its properties; this may lead him to emphasize the way things look from the gymnastic point of view, until, imperceptibly, he is writing something close to a dramatic monologue. Though bothersome to Dr. Johnson, this possibility holds no terror for present generations. On the other hand, the theatrical and grotesque style may be pursued for its own sake, without the least evidence of self-display—with, indeed, a kind of voluptuous self-abnegation. A particularly challenging example here is Richard Crashaw. Scarcely a shadow of dramatic motivation attaches to his writing; he is not in the least like Donne, a displayer of himself. Yet his poetry is perpetually discordant. It makes no effort to soften or rationalize the dissonance of its images and tonalities; rather it takes great pains to search them out and emphasize them. These are, on the whole, dissonances which Herbert's poetry can soften and limit, so that Crashaw's use of them seems, in historical context, particularly gratuitous. The result has been a real splintering of critical opinion. Fragments of Crashaw's poetry appear in a confident little anthology of very bad verse known as *The Stuffed Owl;* the same passages have been subject to elaborate, approving scrutiny by "advanced" critics.

"Decorum of the subject" is also a shallow conception with which to approach Crashaw because it can take no account of the original impulses which drew him consistently to undertake "difficult" subjects. Whether or not there exist subjects which are essentially incongruous, there certainly are combinations of subjects which invite without necessarily involving major incongruity. One of Donne's frequent themes, and Crashaw's primary topic, the yearning for a physical union with the deity, seems almost to defy the possibility of a unified emotional reaction. Its inherent tensions, if pushed very far, must either explode into a joke or balloon into a grotesque. With Donne the topic seems to have remained essentially a metaphor, a bit of conscious hyperbole; when he speaks of God ravishing him or of his amorous soul courting Christ's mild dove, he is using language which as he knows (and explicitly tells us in Holy Sonnet XIII), is exaggerated and "poetic." This is merely an inversion of the sort of semi-blasphemous joke that occurs in "The Relique" where he glances at a comparison between himself and Jesus Christ; if it were anything more than a joke, it would quickly become intolerable. But in Crashaw's verse, Donne's glancing, disjointed vision is converted to a deliberate grating of the nerves, a set of conscious violent discords. The poet unites feelings and thoughts about things which have, indeed, some points of genuine similarity, but between which common sense maintains a degree of antipathy. And the special quality of his fusion is that he does not try to gloss over the latent antipathy, for to sense it is to sense the depth of the feelings that override it. The poet loves God as a baby loves its mother's breast and as a martyr loves the final spear-thrust; he loves God as a gaping wound and a voluptuous mouth, in sophisticated paradox and childish innocence—until all his imagery becomes, as Austin Warren has finely said, "a phantasmagoria . . . of shifting, restless appearances." [4] The unity of opposites, of pain with pleasure, life with death, fruition with denial, assertion with surrender, is his favorite theme. It always involves a degree of incongruity, often of incongruity unresolved, a sense of strain and sometimes of revulsion. It is precisely because he succeeds so well in unifying into one assertion, over the most intense opposition, his "highest" thought and "lowest" feelings, his most physical sensations and his most spiritual aspirations, that conventional "good" taste is sometimes revolted and sometimes amused by Crashaw.

One aspect of Crashaw's "bad taste" is the deliberate injection of a homely word or circumstance amid lofty spiritual reflections. His "financial" metaphors are one example; he likes to speak of shares and dividends, investments and profit-sharing by man in Christ and vice versa. More striking even than this is the conceit in "The Weeper" whereby the Magdalen's tears are imagined as rising, like cream, to the top of a cosmic bottle:

IV
Upwards thou dost weep.
Heavn's bosome drinks the gentle stream.
Where the milky rivers creep,
Thine floats above; and is the cream.
Waters above th' Heav'ns, what they be
We'are taught best by thy TEARS and thee.

[4] *Richard Crashaw* (University, La., 1939), p. 192.

V

Every morn from hence
A brisk Cherub something sippes
Whose sacred influence
Addes sweetnes to his sweetest Lippes.
Then to his musick. And his song
Tasts of this Breakfast all day long.

The transformation of salt tears to milk is queer; raising
the butterfat content to make it cream is odder yet. The
delicacy of "sippes" gives us a slight respite; but the domestic word "breakfast" in congruence with the idea of
aftertaste (the whole image being underlaid by notions of
cud chewing, angelic saliva, and a delicate series of cosmic
belches) would seem to be in the worst possible taste.

How to justify this sort of thing? One may suggest a
kind of appropriateness to the subject matter by saying
that Crashaw is trying to convey the idea of intimacy in
the most intimate terms available to earthly creatures. The
underlying metaphor is perhaps that which calls tears the
milk of human kindness; on this basis the edible aspects
of the image are extended from its center, not imposed
from without. (This is not to say that they could not have
been avoided; it is only that, in a favorite phrase of our own
day, they are perfectly "organic.") The fact, then, that
there is something slightly nauseating about the image may
not be wholly apart from Crashaw's intent; if it were, in
the precise sense, *human* kindness which he was describing,
he might want to show it as incommensurate with the
divine nature.

This sort of speculation is good critical fun and may
even represent more or less accurately a state of mind; but
two considerations inhibit free use of it: first, there is no

evidence, even indirect, to suggest that Crashaw had this sort of thing in mind when he wrote; and, second, if this sort of consideration justifies anything, it justifies everything. Perhaps it is simpler to attribute Crashaw's use of stylistic mannerisms to purely stylistic motives than to invent finespun cosmic proprieties for his justification. But in either event one does not quite know where the critical imputation of "bad taste" can meaningfully lie.

The ultimate test of one's sympathy with Crashaw's taste is found in the isolated and apparently flagrant grotesqueries of the *Divine Epigrams;* where the general economy is so sparse, blossoms of florid feeling and knots of violent contrast assume an almost jungle luxuriance. Note, for instance, the crudity of the epigram "Upon the Body of our Blessed Lord, Naked and Bloody":

> They'have left thee naked, LORD, O that they had!
> This Garment too, I would they had deny'd.
> Thee with thy selfe they have too richly clad;
> Opening the purple wardrobe in thy side.
>   O never could there be garment too good
>   For thee to weare, But this, of thine own blood.

Blood is a royal garment as it is precious, purple, and confers a crown; it clothes many souls otherwise naked and yet represents the supreme sacrifice on the part of Christ. On all these scores the clothes-blood analogy may be made without, in itself, involving "bad taste" or the possibility of grotesque feeling. Only when the poet pushes his image one step further, by referring to the wound from which the blood proceeds as a "wardrobe," do absurdity and the possibility of revulsion enter the poem. Perhaps the oddest thing is the fact that the poem is addressed directly to Christ on the cross; to suggest that his agony is very com fortable and handy for the poet, a veritable bedroom convenience, seems both disturbing and unnecessary. One might argue that there is no other way to convey the combination of sacred, spiritual preciousness with vulgar, social utility—a combination the "naturalness" of which is most clearly betrayed by our conventional expression "*Good* Friday." Yet the very choice of such a theme and such elements as occasions for exercising the witty style may seem in bad taste. Essentially, the judgment must be unitary: if the form is in bad taste, so is the style, so is the subject matter. But what, in this wholesale sense, does "bad taste" mean? Does it imply a judgment that only "harmonious" effects are worth achieving?

Aside from the grating and occasionally dynamic plebeianism, Crashaw also has a rather disturbing way of dealing with orifices, which he likes to dwell upon. The little poem "On the Wounds of Our Crucified Lord" has an almost surrealist way with a wound:

> O these wakefull wounds of thine!
> Are they Mouthes? or are they eyes?
> Be they mouthes, or be they eyne,
> Each bleeding part some one supplies.
>
> Lo, a mouth! whose full bloom'd lips
> At too deare a rate are roses:
> Lo, a blood-shot eye! that weeps,
> And many a cruell teare discloses.
>
> O thou that on this foot hast laid
> Many a kisse, and many a teare,
> Now thou shalt have all repaid
> What soe're thy charges were.

> This foot hath got a mouth and lips
> To pay the sweet summe of thy kisses,
> To pay thy teares, an eye that weeps,
> Instead of teares, such gems as this is.
>
> The difference only this appears,
> (Nor can the change offend)
> The debt is paid in Ruby-teares
> Which thou in Pearles did lend.

The vulgarity of the bargain ("too deare a rate" and "whatsoe're thy charges were" are touches worthy of Cowley) counterpoints the extravagant wound imagery; the wounds which become mouths to kiss and eyes to weep have distinctly traumatic overtones, and the sensual cherishing of wounds plays off very finely against the counting out of a money debt. If we resist the poet's imaginative unification of his feelings about Christ on the grounds that kissing wounds is unlovely and perverse and counting out change is vulgar, we may seem to quarrel with a conceivable central point, that love of Christ includes all extremes and reconciles all contraries. The white tear of innocence is repaid by the red blood of anguish; "nor can the change offend"—or, for that matter, the combination. Under the circumstances, "bad taste" seems an irrelevant notion, and the door is open to any sort of violent incongruity which can be yoked (preferably in the name of religion but really in the interests of any strong feeling) to a higher unity. The difficulty of drawing incongruities together thus becomes a measure of the loftiness of the impulses which unite them; bad taste has become a form of good taste.

Crashaw himself never carried the revolting aspects of his imagery farther than in the epigram on Luke 11, "Blessed be the paps which thou hast sucked":

> Suppose he had been tabled at thy Teates,
> Thy hunger feels not what he eates:
> Hee'l have his Teat e're long, a bloody one,
> The mother then must suck the son.

The poet here comes close to a direct statement that the Incarnation was a revolting joke on Jesus and Mary; incest, perversion, cannibalism, and the extra incongruity of "tabled at thy Teates" make the quatrain a little gem of incrusted grotesquerie. Most striking of all is the neat, swift, rather pleased tone of the antithesis; in notions not only lovely but familiar, it seems, horrid possibilities may lurk. Certainly in this poem Crashaw can hardly have intended anything but a nasty twist to the spiritual-carnal relation.

Equally outrageous to the conventional sense of decorum but comic in its startling release of inappropriate connotations is the famous stanza XIX of "The Weeper":

> And now where're he strayes
> Among the Galilean mountaines,
> Or more unwellcome wayes,
> He's follow'd by two faithfull fountaines;
> Two walking baths; two weeping motions;
> Portable, and compendious oceans.

This deservedly famous stanza reminds one of nothing so much as a landscape by Dali. The Magdalen's grief is grotesque; it distorts her out of all resemblance to humanity. The human features as they distort and break down into tears have usually been accounted ugly; her tears, as they transcend ordinary grief, transcend ordinary ugliness and absurdity. It is not, as grief, even especially acceptable to Christ. The "more unwellcome wayes" are of course those leading to his Crucifixion, but in conjunction with the cumulative absurdities at the end of the stanza they may also be taken to suggest Christ's attitude toward his forlorn follower. Her grief is helpless, uncontrollable, pathetic—yet portable and abridged because of her absurd humanity. One laughs at the images, but one squirms under them too; and this effect can, if Crashaw's art is art and not accident, be taken as meaningful without exactly being called "expressive." The whole technique of loosely, floridly extended metaphor seems to culminate in this stanza, which is ridiculous, of course, as an operatic duet between a pair of duelists is ridiculous; the art is developed beyond and in defiance of nature. But its absurdity can be seen as true to a sort of feeling, a manner, a style; and if the feeling does not assert itself irresistibly over the difficulties imposed by flesh, blood, and a sense of humor, irresistible triumph is not, perhaps, what is intended. The feeling is to be colored by a radical sense of absurdity, even to be derived, by a queer kind of negative emphasis, from the absurdity, as if the absurdity were somehow a guarantee of the point of view from which alone a grief so ghastly could seem absurd. A Christian poet, at least, can scarcely be blamed for assuming, and asking his readers to assume for the moment, a definition of reality which includes more than the humanly demonstrable; and how to suggest such a reality if not through the feelings imagined as appropriate to it?

Severe judges with nineteenth-century tastes used to cite

passages from "The Weeper" and similar poems as evidence of Crashaw's complete inability to criticize his own work; Ruth Wallerstein, intent on rehabilitating Crashaw, undertook to minimize them as youthful follies, soon outgrown. But Austin Warren, picking up the old-fashioned view with a difference, was the first to suggest that they are the product of a different sort of taste than conventional "good" taste, not failures to resemble Marvell's "Garden," but poems formed on a different model altogether.[5] Miss Wallerstein's compromise was charitable but scarcely seems compatible with the personal chronology of Richard Crashaw; after all, the 1648 version of "The Weeper" added the stanza on "walking baths," and as Crashaw died early in 1649, one can scarcely dismiss the stanza as immature work. The purple-wardrobe epigram was first published in *Steps to the Temple* (1646), only three years before his death, and reprinted in 1652, along with the "financial" "Caritas Nimia" and an especially visceral and sanguinary song, "Upon the Bleeding Crucifix." Crashaw's taste, it appears, developed neither toward nor away from the grotesque metaphor which we consider in "bad taste"; it simply included an area of "very bad taste" within a larger area of "inoffensive taste" and rose occasionally to something we can call "impeccable taste," always provided our standards of taste are purely conventional. In less colored words, Crashaw's images sometimes contain much of the grotesque (plebeian or visceral), sometimes little, sometimes none at all. What they contain they subordinate to

[5] George Saintsbury, *A History of Elizabethan Literature* (London, 1887), p. 369; Wallerstein, *Richard Crashaw* (Madison, Wis., 1935), *passim*; Warren, ch. iii.

a purer harmony sometimes easily, sometimes with difficulty, sometimes only by violent imputation.

That metaphysical devotional poetry of this order involves two radically different sorts of taste rather than two
stages in an individual's poetic development may be seen
by turning to an example of modern devotional baroque.
It is perhaps too early to tell if the so-called "Religious
Sonnets" of Dylan Thomas will survive, or on what terms—
whether because or in spite of their taste, because supported by more conventional poems, or under impulse
of their own buoyancy or their own obscurity. But it is
clear that enjoyment of poems which describe Christ as a
"hang-nail cracked from Adam," the angel Gabriel as a
cowboy, and God the Father as an "old cock from no-
wheres," depends on a taste which is not only metaphysical
but includes a tolerance for the baroque and the grotesque.

A great deal about Thomas' sonnets is interesting, aside
from their taste. Technically they are a rare treat—driving,
energetic, complex, and lawless. They sometimes accept
off rhyme or assonance as the equivalent of rhyme and
feminine endings as the equivalent of assonance; sometimes
they forget recognizable rhymes altogether. Their basic
rhyme pattern is set by the first sonnet of the ten, if my
ear serves me, as abcbacdedefgfg; but the c-c rhyme,
originally as weak as Adam-scream, soon fades altogether,
and some of the other rhymes are forgotten when convenient. The punctuation of particular sonnets is odd; a
semicolon, particularly, seems to belong one line down in
I, 2 and II, 6; and a question mark in IV, 6 cries out to be
made a comma. The grammar as written often defies pars-
ing, the reference of pronouns is chaotic (I's, you's, he's

and we's being used without either distinct or consistent points of reference), and the imagery, always violent and often grotesque, is based in turn on castration, Homer, the Apocalypse, Egyptology, pastorals, the Wild West, and playing cards. The point of view is explicitly that at which Crashaw only hinted—that Incarnation represents a vicious joke played by a malicious God on Christ, Mary, and mankind.

That the topic is appropriate to a metaphysical style there is no denying; indeed, the metaphysical mode is inherently sympathetic to the theme, for its essence is the mingling, under stress of an overriding emotion, of two disparate spheres amid deliberate overtones of aesthetic as well as ethical anguish. But the blinding closeness of Thomas' contrasts has not many parallels in literature; for intensity seems to be the chief value of his style, and the effect is brilliantly achieved by a close, compact grinding together of images under the impulse of a steady, rhythmic pulse and a taut, heavily end-stopped line. Thomas evidently intends, like Crashaw, a chaotic mingling of many different sorts of anguish, a phantasmagoria of pain and grief. To achieve this end he uses language percussively, like a pianist playing with his forearms, creating a furious, barbaric, dissonant clangor which has all sorts of intensity but not a great deal of structure. Thus, though he has imposed several sorts of uniformity on his material, there is almost nothing about it which could be described as unity. Images are repeated, varied, punned upon, transformed, and trodden down by other images; but there is no one logical or emotional development which exercises control over all others.

In this respect, Thomas' sonnets contrast strikingly with

Donne's, or even with Crashaw's poetic style. The searching, darting movement of Donne's thought is proverbial; though the motivating and directing force is generally temperament, the shape it assumes is logical. Though it often pursues two or more logical directions at once, it rarely defies logical possibilities for long, certainly never exaggerates that defiance without qualification or ultimate resolution in a larger logical unity. So with Crashaw; through the movement of images is more emotional than logical and so the texture of the verse is looser, the images cluster and exalt themselves in a clear pattern of responses to the intensity of the poet's feeling. But when, for example, Thomas in "Sonnet IV" undertakes a series of outrageous paradoxical absurdities in the manner of "Go and catch a falling star," they neither come from anywhere nor lead to anything. The one assertion which seems to derive is the poet's vision of the Resurrection after the Entombment:

> Corset the boneyards for a crooked boy?
> Button your bodice on a hump of splinters,
> My camel's eyes will needle through the shroud.[6]

Of any other poet it would be ridiculous to say he has nothing to lead up to but the Resurrection. But here one is faced with a Resurrection which occurs ("Sonnet IV") before the Crucifixion ("Sonnet VIII") and which is not built into an event of stature anyhow. When his camel's eyes have needled through the shroud, Thomas does not see anything in particular. He goes on to discuss, with an orphic absence of verbs, the process of seeing; but he says nothing of the central actor or incident:

[6] Copyright 1952, 1953 by Dylan Thomas. Reprinted by permission of New Directions.

Love's reflection of the mushroom features,
Stills snapped by night in the bread-sided field,
Once close-up smiling in the wall of pictures,
Arc-lamped thrown back upon the cutting flood.

Whether one looks at "Sonnet IV" by itself or as one of a sequence, it trails off without either conclusion or attachment; and the accumulated absurdities of the first seven lines lead to no such resolution as their rising energy seems to be preparing for.

The fact is that the sonnets are fragmentary in much the same way as "The Weeper," but more radically; they lack not only over-all form but defined relations between parts. One mark of this lack is a vagueness about the attempts at explication; most of them suffer from a hesitant, either-or tone deriving from the fact that the relations between elements—between, say, the bagpipe-breasted sirens and the Crucifixion, or the white bear quoting Virgil and two-gunned Gabriel—has been defined by the critic, not the poet. "Maybe Thomas means this or perhaps that." The implication is that it does not matter much which alternative one chooses; and since, in a sense, Thomas himself has made no definite choice, it isn't really up to the reader to choose either. All this is well and good; a poet may certainly enrich his poem by meaning two things at once, but he will certainly confuse it by meaning sixteen things at once, without making clear the relation between them. The most capacious and unstrained form of unity that can be seen is undoubtedly the best—and this it is undoubtedly the reader's, or the critic's, responsibility to discover. It is even conceivable that the full meaning of a poem may be understood only by looking at it in several distinct, even incompatible ways, successively. No price is too high to pay for genuine richness. But a multitude of hazily related, or unrelated, particulars may produce not the impression of richness but that of monotony. And then if the whole structural unity of the poem is resolved into a single, drumming, extravagant antithesis, along with all hope for variety of effect, the greater part of one's notion of structural decorum must go by the board. There are very few poems in the canon which give such an effect of blind, swirling energy unrelated to a total structure as these "Religious Sonnets" of Dylan Thomas. They remind one of the paintings of Jackson Pollock—a vortex of energy, totally unmechanical, immediate and violent, with all the raw ends of the creator's nerves showing, yet not really distinguishable one from the other.

Is it a defensible aesthetic position to say that so long as each individual section of his poem is built on sufficiently violent and intensive contrasts the poet need provide no structure of mood, tone, imagery, temporal order, or grammatical assertion? The distinctions here are quantitative, not absolute; but there certainly comes a point where confused poems seem to represent the best approach to confusion and dull novels the most exquisite expression of dullness. This is the imitative fallacy with a vengeance; in matters of dullness and confusion we condemn it easily enough, but when questions of grotesque and incongruous taste are at issue our standards somehow become less rigid. Perhaps we have really learned that there are more universes to be inhabited than are dreamt of in any one philosophy. But the world of those who divide taste into "good" and "bad" has strictly unitary implications. To be applied at all, the concepts will have to be applied wholesale, and within a rather rigid conventional framework.

If the central theme of a poem is not subject to the imputation of bad taste, no meaning can attach to a condemnation of ornaments which may be perfectly appropriate to, and expressive of, that theme. When the theme becomes incongruity itself, we are close to a no-man's-land where all standards of taste are conditional on one's "taste" for the actual thing being experienced. The real complaint against metaphysical poetry of the intense and unresolved variety is not that it assumes one sort of taste as a touchstone in opposition to all others but that it casts a doubt on the general relevance of *any* single standard of taste. It makes explicit that dependence of the poem on the reader's imaginative experience which is only implicit in conventional poetry, and it does so by presuming a special condition in the reader that is too widespread to be called private but a good deal less than universal.

Certainly there are concepts of the world within which nightmare and disorder qualified by intellectual energy are the only conceivable terms of vision. Poetry need not *express* such a chaotic concept of the universe; it may simply accept and operate within that conception. In these terms, metaphysical poetry may be but one aspect of a baroque aesthetic which, in literature as in plastic art, stakes everything on a vision of space, tension, disparity, and centrifugal dislocation. If it is but one aspect of something as widespread as a style, perhaps the discordant metaphysical manner needs no justification at all, beyond the characteristic experiences of the human mind itself. To see the world as degenerating from a previous order is as natural and probably as correct as to suppose that it is progressing toward a new one; some sort of vision of deterioration, combined with an impulse to order, is implied in the metaphysical style. There is a pleasure to be had, not merely from dramatic opposition, but from a sense of the mind's limitations being actually enlarged by holding onto dissolving solidities in a void. Form, that is, may be intentional as well as actual. But even this is overstatement; form need not really be actively intentional at all. It may be implicit in the undeclared circumstance of a single point of view, or in two contrasting points of view which the poet drives against the unity of a single grammatical assertion. Then it is more or less "open," of course. Our natural state as readers is Periclean repose, to be sure; but metaphysical poetry reminds us that this repose may be merely an uneasy, momentary balance of growth and decay, and the best health of which we are capable simply that which is built on the warfare of conflicting maladies. Once we have accepted this view, poetry is a fever chart; the more metaphysical it is as poetry, and the more open as metaphysical poetry, the more it reveals our natural state and offers us the capacity for real health—which is nothing less than the state of true and proper "di-vision." Both the self and the various decorums built on more or less unified concepts of selfhood then become irrelevant; bad taste is simply what interferes with vision. In place of "harmonious" virtues and "dissonant" faults, concepts like intensity, profundity, scope, and relevance come to govern. They are vague, but not impossibly so; a fuller discussion of them will be delayed till the end of this volume.

∽ VII ∽

Swift and Kafka:
Satiric Incongruity and the
Inner Defeat of the Mind

ALTHOUGH the world of satire is traditionally a world
of disorganization and dislocation, it is typically seen by
an eye which knows something better and which can emphasize the disorder by contrasting it with an understood
or remembered order, a standard of excellence somehow
known or implied. For this reason, mock heroic is one of
the natural modes of satire. It has sometimes been observed,
however, that the effect of constant mock-heroic juxtaposition is to exalt Dullness, or Duplicity, into a heroic quality.
It has not so often been emphasized that satire may also
dissolve the order which ostensibly serves as a foil for disorder, leaving the author and reader bewildered amid a
glare of glittering, cutting incongruities. An example of
such satire, many-faceted and sharp-edged, is Jonathan
Swift's *Tale of a Tub*, with its appendages *The Battle of
the Books* and *A Discourse Concerning the Mechanical
Operation of the Spirit*. It is a bold, hard, angular engine,

which still cannot be carelessly handled without danger of a slash.

Swift's hydra-headed satire is in many respects a work peculiar to its time. The ancients-versus-moderns controversy, around which much of the satire is grouped, was strictly ephemeral. The sort of reading which Swift's book implies (like that which it attacks) was already outmoded; important objects of his satire, the fanatic preachers, were essentially creatures of the dying century. The very manner of the book which is shapeless, rhapsodic, stuffed with learning and authorial crotchets, clearly derives from that wonderful, crazy century which had produced *The Anatomy of Melancholy* and William Prynne, *Pseudodoxia Epidemica* and the Fifth Monarchy Men—not to mention *Don Quixote*. Thus, the "corruptions in Religion and Learning" against which the author leveled his lance were in outward form at least those of a bygone or bygoing day. But *A Tale of a Tub* is not to be understood as a mechanical derivation from the social circumstances of the time, much less as a collection of intellectual factors piled together in a basket of "moral realism." If there is one thing clear about Swift, it is the high tension at which his mind operated, its impatient energy, its tendency to dominate and use intellectual materials. His prose, even when polished to a high gloss, is always muscular; and its muscles are always at work. His jokes, his games, his private languages and little societies, his paradoxes, and all the dramatic contrasts of his life, which furnish such rich material for the biographer, the dramatist, and the purveyor of avowed or unavowed fiction, are also evidence of an emotional and intellectual turbulence which made him the theater of an endless struggle. He did not develop placidly, one more chain-linked bacillus on a neo-Stoic string; his mind was torn by agonies of conflict before he possessed the ideological framework to explain or the symbolic dress in which to clothe it; and his book is the expression quite as much of a temperament as of an era. One illustration of this fact derives from a contrast between *A Tale of a Tub* and *Gulliver's Travels*. *Gulliver* is much the more polished performance; it has a clarity of outline and concept which is scarcely broken, and a steady progression of symbols. The ragged edges of Swift's fury have been buried within a deliberately smooth, deceptive surface, like broken glass set in concrete. *A Tale of a Tub*, on the other hand, is all hard, raw, self-assured, and fantastic in its angled bravado. It lacks a good deal in scheme and symbols, in shape and structure—not that the book fails to exploit its own lacks in these regards; because it is committed to so little, it makes all the more capital of its freedom to mock structure as well as lack of structure—but for this very reason it exposes more nakedly the bare bones and quivering nerves of Swift's logical and emotional conflicts. One cannot help feeling that in *A Tale of a Tub* Swift was reaching into the deepest, and most immediate, background of frustrations, which were partly psychological and partly philosophical but which determined and involved his whole existence as an individual. If his reading, as he declared, was all fresh in his head, so also were his angers and humiliations; and out of the two he created a work altogether original—one which he flung on the counters of a shopkeeping nation with the rage of a man who finds he has been handed a counterfeit coin.

One of the key scenes of *A Tale of a Tub*, which gave contemporary opinion one of its rudest shocks, shows Peter

establishing for his brothers the doctrine of transubstantia-
tion. He carves them a couple of pieces of bread and pretends that it is mutton. After some discussion:

"What, then, My Lord," replied the first, "it seems this is a
shoulder of mutton all this while." "Pray, sir," says Peter, "eat
your vittles and leave off your impertinence, if you please, for
I am not disposed to relish it at present." But the other could
not forbear, being overprovoked at the affected seriousness
of Peter's countenance. "By G--, My Lord," said he, "I can
only say that to my eyes and fingers and teeth and nose it seems
to be nothing but a crust of bread." Upon which, the second
put in his word: "I never saw a piece of mutton in my life so
nearly resembling a slice from a twelve-penny loaf." "Look ye,
gentlemen," cries Peter in a rage, "to convince you what a
couple of blind, positive, ignorant, wilful puppies you are,
I will use but this plain argument: By G--, it is true, good,
natural mutton as any in Leaden-Hall market, and G-- con-
found you both eternally, if you offer to believe otherwise."

Peter's outburst of hysterical rage is in the dominant key of
A Tale of a Tub; like the weaver of the Preface, he speaks
in the thick, choked accents of violent fury—a fury which
at once perpetrates and exposes a gross, outrageous fraud.
If we suppose one of the central concerns of the book to be
the discovery and rejection of fraud, it will appear as the
expression of a temperament and a function only sec-
ondarily determined by social circumstance and prudential
motives. Swift denounces in *A Tale of a Tub* the two forms
of fraud and corruption that time and circumstance had
rendered most obnoxious. But the relish with which he
goes about his denunciations and the lengths to which he
carries them express a purely personal need. So much intense and peculiar pleasure seemed to lie in the uprooting

of deceit and corruption that truth and health, even if found, could only have appeared as a disappointment.

But this denunciation of fraud, while an overriding concern of the author, is not the principle on which *A Tale of a Tub* is organized. Neither can the book be wholly described as an exposé of the innocent who pretends to be its author, important as this theme doubtless is. Although its surface is flauntingly and defiantly incoherent, *A Tale of a Tub* is, I think, chiefly held together by a pair of images which achieve explicit statement only in a fragment never fully incorporated in the book itself, though constantly associated with it. *A Discourse Concerning the Mechanical Operation of the Spirit* places in opposition two concepts, the machine and the spirit, which had been deeply involved in the history of the seventeenth century and in the experience of Jonathan Swift. These two concepts are also, and singularly, themes common to the story of Jack, Peter, and Martin, to the digressions, and to the (no less than five) comments prefatory to *A Tale of a Tub*. The wind and the machine are of central, summary importance to Swift, his book, and his time; he is equally hostile to both, and, though he generally uses one to mock the other, he sometimes plays audaciously at identifying them.

The "spirit" for which Swift feels such antipathy is a quality that takes many forms; in one of his formal moments the author distinguishes manifestations of the spirit according to their origin, as the products of divine inspiration, diabolic possession, inner motives (imagination, anger, fear, grief, pain, etc.), or mechanical manipulation. But the spirit shows itself in all sorts of ways which cannot be so strictly catalogued: in self-importance (the greedy importunity of the bookseller, the lofty airs of the starving author, the alleged delusions of Descartes); in dogmatic ignorance; in esoteric doctrines, numerology, and elaborate word spinnings; in the deliberate vagaries of digression counterdigressed by digression; in the pretensions of the modern age over the ancients; in the interpretive triumph of the three brothers over their father's will; in military conquests; in the lucky victory of the madman over the sane.

What precisely is the spirit? It is agitated air, "a redundancy of vapors," whether denominated enthusiasm, hysteria, or inspiration; its exponents are the learned Aeolists, a set of inflated gapers after air; it is the effective cause of conquests and systems, of faction and madness. Its normal seat is in the lungs, the belly, and the genitals; denied adequate expression here, it may rise to the brain and afflict that organ with a vapor. What the difference is between overt, acknowledged madness and those forms of undeclared madness which are socially rewarded Swift half offers to make clear; but the explanation dissolves into a *Hiatus in MS,* and the satiric edge of his wit is turned against all forms of wind, because all make, or are capable of making, man turbulent and fantastic.

For the brain in its natural position and state of serenity disposeth its owner to pass his life in the common forms, without any thought of subduing multitudes to his own power, his reasons, or his visions; and the more he shapes his understanding by the pattern of human learning, the less he is inclined to form parties after his particular notions, because that instructs him in his private infirmities, as well as in the stubborn ignorance of the people. But when a man's fancy gets astride on his reason, when imagination is at cuffs with the senses, and common understanding as well as common sense is kickt out of doors, the first proselyte he makes is himself, and when that is once compass'd the difficulty is not so great in bringing over others—a strong delusion always operating from without as vigorously as from within.

The function and title of the book are themselves involved in the image of the spirit as an explosive "redundancy of vapors"; the wits of the age having been found to threaten the church and state, a project for diverting their energies was sought; and as whales are given a tub to play with in order to divert them from attacking a ship, so *A Tale of a Tub* was produced to divert the wits who, puffed up with modern presumption and armed with sharp weapons from Hobbes's *Leviathan*, were becoming dangerous. Thus the mechanical excitement and mechanical manipulation of wind into one social form or another become the predominant images of Swift's satire; and while no more precise definitions are made of the sort of wind or the sort of social form satirized, the nature of the wind or spirit particularly is pretty clear. The weight of Swift's attack lies against the private spirit, the irrational personal conviction of logical rightness, physical authority, or spiritual justification.

How heavy that weight lies may be realized when one notes the vast arsenal of satiric weapons with which Swift assaults the spirit and its manifestations. He persistently implies that all forms of inspiration are of the two lower varieties—neither divine nor diabolic in origin, but the product of imaginative self-indulgence or of deliberate mechanical manipulation, of lust, filth, greed, or folly. Thus he explains an imperial conquest as the effect of an unsatisfied erection, imputes pulpit eloquence to sexual excitement, and bitterly derogates all forms of enthusiasm by equating the winds which puff them up.

Mists arise from the earth, steams from dunghills, exhalations from the sea, and smoke from fire; yet all clouds are the same in composition as well as consequences, and the fumes issuing from a jakes will furnish as comely and useful a vapor as incense from an altar.

All clouds are the same, in composition as well as consequences; that is to say, all clouds and vapors are degrading to human nature. Sex and excrement are the unremitting associates of spiritual inspiration, the mechanical foundations on which enthusiasms are founded and to which they inevitably revert. No more terrible and degrading association is open to Swift's imagination. The preacher whose canting reaches its height in an act of physical orgasm; the prince whose urge to conquest derives from unexpended semen; the Aeolists, who worship in circles "with every man a pair of bellows applied to his neighbor's breech"; the female priests, ancient and modern, "whose organs were understood to be better disposed for the admission of those oracular gusts"; the Aeolian admiration for belching (especially, by a fine touch of art, through the nose) and for the ancient institution of barrels, from which air is introduced, through funnels, to the breech—all bespeak an aversion which, for Swift, amounted almost to phobia. The similarity that Swift affects to discover between Jack and Peter, the church of Geneva and that of Rome, is founded upon their mutual susceptibility to wind, "the phrenzy and the spleen of both having the same foundation." And for Swift no more repulsive view of the human species is conceivable than that of the inflated and presumptuous Aeolist.

But though the primary edge of the *Tale of a Tub* is directed against the windy Aeolists and their most picturesque exemplars, the fanatic sectarians, the book's emotional structure is not that of an author secure in his possession of "that natural position and state of security" which enables a man "to pass his life in the common forms." One could look for no better example of the placid, adjusted man than Swift's great enemy William Wotton, whose reaction to the *Tale of a Tub* was one of unqualified horror. Although Swift's theological blasphemies may have been exaggerated, his raging contempt for the whole race of moderns can scarcely be overstated; and surely this implies, on the face of it, a considerable contempt for the "common forms." Indeed, a treatise so fantastic, sardonic, and derisive as *A Tale of a Tub* could scarcely culminate in a calm conformity; the expenditure of so much nervous ingenuity merely to endorse the "common forms" would be at the least a paradox, akin to that by which the fourth book of *Gulliver* may be read as the most passionate denunciation of passion ever penned. Undoubtedly *A Tale of a Tub* partakes of this paradoxical character; and Swift (or at least his author-mask) is explicit in his recognition of the fact:

Even I myself, the author of these momentous truths, am a person whose imaginations are hard-mouthed, and exceedingly disposed to run away with his reason, which I have observed from long experience to be a very light rider, and easily shook off.

But there is a further complexity to *A Tale of a Tub*; the problem is not simply that the satiric attack includes, in some measure, as its object the author himself; it is that the point of view from which one satire is launched is itself the object of a second attack, and the "common forms" into which the sane and ordinary mind placidly fits are ridiculed under the aspect of a machine.

The story of Jack, Peter, and Martin, the Calvinist, Roman Catholic, and Lutheran churches, is ostensibly a story in which the reasonable *via media* of the church of England is upheld against the superstition of Rome and the crude, violent inspirations of the sects. The satire upon the philosophers of wind, likewise, tends to support the reasonable, common-sense judgment of the enlightened, unprejudiced few. But Martin's placid responses to Jack are ridiculed as the tricky devices of a cunning debater; and the three machines, of ladder, pulpit, and stage itinerant, are presented as the types of all modern authorship—grotesque devices of elevation to facilitate the puffing of air into a multitude. Here once more the author introduces himself and his own book within the framework of the satire, describing his present production as a work of the stage itinerant; and indeed, there is no evident principle (save obiter dictum) by which any work or author could be exempted from the satire. Swift's hatred of the moderns (which is a principle more vital to him than love of the ancients) seems to allow no room for exceptions, no escape from primitive presumption and mechanical craft.

Not only is the machine a frequent device for controlling the escape of redundant vapor (as most schemes of religion and government resemble tubs in being "hollow and dry and empty and noisy and wooden and given to rotation"); machines may also be used to excite the more pretentious and windy spiritual activities. Under the cover of spiritual aims, carnal energies are gratified; by mechanical devices, excess spiritual wind is diverted into useful channels. The relation of wind and machine is reciprocal; schemes and projects are the mere complements of fanaticism and enthusiasm. This of course is the history of Protestant sectarianism in a nutshell; the energy of the saints, diverted to secular projects and mechanical improvements, gave rise to that eighteenth-century outlook for which philosophy and religion are both in different ways too exalted names but which is very adequately described as Franklinism. The application of religious zeal to business ends is the essence of Franklinism, as of the "modern spirit" which Swift hated. Because his Tory principles involved a deep-seated preference for the slow, traditional forms of a landed aristocracy over the sharper, more competitive, turbulent, and individualist ways of the money men, Swift despised all Getting Ahead; and he hated individual passion or appetite more even than wind and machines because it was the determining agent of both.

Standing apart from "discipline-directed" as from "system-directed" man, Swift saw, I think, a good deal deeper into the human dilemma of the day than any of the formal philosophers of his time. Shaftesbury and Mandeville, for example, disagreed as to the motive power of the social machine; did benevolence or greed make it tick? But neither dreamed of repudiating the view that society at its best is a clockwork which absorbs and makes use of the various motives of men. While Locke was rendering Christianity reasonable in terms of a mechanical philosophy and while Berkeley was quietly gathering the spiritual principle into a defiant solipsism, Swift, instead of trying to reconcile the alternatives of spirit and matter or to choose between them, made it is his concern to repudiate them both. He figures, then, as a man utterly deprived of those usual philosophical supports and props of belief with which the average man surrounds himself. Swift's pride is a particularly brilliant, because partly inadequate, substitute for a system; had it been more formalized, he would never have defied with such savage success his own prescriptions against scribbling. Standing apart from his society, and with special horror from those who had rebelled against it, Swift achieved at bitter expense an especially acute and individual insight into it. If his performance seems sometimes to partake of levitation or puppetry because he gets along with so much less positive, constructive belief than his contemporaries found decent, a modern eye may find in that fact at least one measure of his achievement.

The cry of "destructiveness" has long echoed about the *Tale of a Tub;* and though it may not be as damning as William Wotton and F. R. Leavis suppose, it is probably a valid cry. If there are positive teachings lurking in the book, one is hard put to know what they are. Certainly "integrity" is no solution to the question of what Swift is inculcating. Integrity or moral realism is what Swift started with and never abandoned, even though it led him toward the most terrible of all conclusions, nihilism. Whether he ever actually formulated this conclusion may be debated; if he did not, only the hard and brilliant façade of his egotism saved him from it. For the evident tendency of his thought, which builds only to undermine and undermines in so many different directions, leaves as a shield against nihilism only that arrogance of temper which first led him toward it.

As to the precise nature of these temperamental impulses and their conditioning, one can do no more than speculate. Clearly, the frigid isolation of Swift's political and social thought corresponds in some measure to the alienation of his personal situation. Orphanage, genteel poverty, a temperamental horror of intimacy, the peculiar dilemmas of Anglo-Irish Protestantism, and the general debacle of enthusiasms political, literary, and religious—all no doubt contributed. But these are general considerations. As for the precise determining qualities of Swift's individual mind, it must always be a curious, abstracted argument why the same vapor produces such peculiar effects upon different individuals; and perhaps no better answer can be found than a *Hiatus in MS.* In any event, the result can scarcely be mistaken. Neither in the individual nor in the group, neither in the "common forms" nor out of them does Swift see any tolerable, let alone easy, way toward the good life.

Individual conscience is an engine of individual greed; systems and conquests are engines of collective greed; the way of the world is an engine of universal greed; and the most unexceptionable virtues are, as perverted by the inescapable corruptness of human nature, mere façades for filth, fraud, and lust. The account of a clothes religion, which satirizes man as an empty, hollow exterior (in strict counterpoint to the Aeolists, who are despised as windy, shapeless enthusiasts), culminates in a series of ironic definitions:

To instance no more: is not religion a cloak; honesty a pair of shoes worn out in the dirt; self-love a surtout; vanity a shirt; and conscience a pair of breeches; which, though a cover for lewdness as well as nastiness, is easily slipt down for the service of both?

Although the ironies of this passage are many and complexly wrought, its decisive point seems directed against those who judge of men by their exterior—against the shallowness and emptiness of life as seen from the outside only. But this was in fact something of Swift's own position; he had, as we have seen, a profound sense that the deeper one looked into human nature the more corruption one was likely to uncover; and the greatest achievement of his ironic stoicism was the suggestion that men must be trained not to look beyond the surface of things, so that they might thereby attain to "the sublime and refined point of felicity called the possession of being well deceived, the serene peaceful state of being a fool among knaves."

Here, too, are ironies galore. By looking only at the surface of things one remains happy and a fool; by delving into the arcana one becomes miserable (for what one finds is ugly) and a knave (for obscure knowledge gives rise to flimflam systems). The structure of Swift's assertion here, as frequently elsewhere, involves an ascending rhetorical series culminating in a deliberate anticlimax, an act of destruction. Such is, for example, his metaphorical description of wisdom:

It is a fox, who after long hunting will at last cost you the pains to dig out. 'Tis a cheese, which by how much the richer has the thicker, the homelier, and the coarser coat, and whereof to a judicious palate the maggots are best. 'Tis a sack-posset, wherein the deeper you go you will find it the sweeter. Wisdom is a hen, whose cackling we must value and consider because it is attended with an egg. But then, lastly, 'tis a nut which unless you choose with judgment may cost you a tooth and pay you with nothing but a worm.

This comparative characterization may of course be taken in some degree seriously; but the homeliness of the imagery speaks another language. Maggots, worms, and broken teeth are scarcely the appropriate rewards for a search after knowledge which is being wholeheartedly recommended. One of Swift's notes on a pretended gap in the manuscript speaks a much more direct language: "Here is another defect in the manuscript, but I think the author did wisely and that the matter which thus strained his faculties was not worth a solution, and it were well if all metaphysical cobweb problems were no otherwise answered." Dark authors are thus absurd on one side, as are superficial writers on the other; and in fact the two follies complement one another. A true "modern" (that is, "fool") pretends deep learning to conceal his ignorance of plain truths; and for the particular benefit of such our innocent author has prepared his *New Help of Smatterers; or, the Art of Being Deep-learned and Shallow-read.*

Satire of the credulous followed by satire of the skeptical; satire directed against the windy interiors and then against the hollow exteriors of men; satire directed against the machine and against the wind which fills it; satire so double-edged and double-directed leaves very little ground exempted from satire of one sort or another. Swift does not do anything so placid as teeter indecisively between two satiric points of view; he is the theater of a battle, the register of furiously conflicting tensions, where all thought and feeling is an area of dispute. The Toryism of Swift thus surpasses (or sinks beneath) the prudential principles of a Clarendon or a Harley. Swift is a psychological rather than a political Tory—a statement which takes us a good way toward the notion that the essence of his thinking was not Tory at all. At the very least, we may distinguish two sorts of Toryism, the one prudential, political, traditional, unprincipled, and creative, the other emotional, psychological, individual, dogmatic, and destructive.

The word "Tory" and the usual concept of Toryism

have oddly little to do with a point of view so austerely and complexly and self-defeatingly individual as Swift's. It is a paradox often remarked that the fury with which he undertook to bottle up every last outlet of individualism brought Swift to the very outposts of crankiness, eccentricity, and overt insanity; his rage for order was such that it surpassed at once the limits of politics and later the limits of art, till it became unhesitatingly a question of his own individual existence. The psychological quality of Swift's Toryism derived from the fact that for him order was rage and torment, not an existing principle; and from this fact was determined the whole series of uneasy ambivalences (toward love and authority, toward mankind and himself, toward filth and cleanliness, toward past and present) which make up the fascination of his personality.

Generally speaking, the seventeenth century fell into psychology as into an ambush. Locke's experience summarized in capsule form that of the entire century. Setting out to dispute concerning a substantive matter, he and his friends quickly found themselves at a complete stand, unable to determine anything until they had come to an agreement concerning human understanding and the degree of certainty to which it could properly aspire. Swift fell into the same pit and never succeeded in getting out of it, perhaps because he never wanted to. But he made of it a kingdom of brilliant fantasy within which his own role, now as supreme monarch and now as tortured outcast, never ceased to be central and absorbing. Not only was his symbolic role within the fantasy strikingly dual, but so also was his personal role as creator of it. He was both the prisoner of his imagination and the jailer of it. His books served both to give Swift a revenge upon society and to ingratiate him

with it. ("They may talk of the *you know what*," he wrote
to Stella, referring guardedly to the *Tale of a Tub*, "but,
gad, if it had not been for that, I should never have been
able to get the access I have had.") His increasing use of
symbols is itself a mark of this dualism; for the symbol, as
allegory and object, looks two ways and exists in an essential tension even when, by a kind of stereoptical vision,
object and idea seem to be fused. One's awareness of symbolic writing is never merely direct, and a particularly
striking quality of Swift's symbolism is the duplicity of its
effect. Among any group of readers there will always be
some who find Swift hilarious and others who find only a
deep sense of pain and misery. There will be some who
giggle and some who wince. Neither of these responses is
the proper one; neither is even preferable. Both are legitimate, and so intimately connected that they may exist
within the same person almost at the same time. The comedy of the digression on madness is close to hysteria; as we
laugh, we cringe. If one of the symbolic acts of *A Tale of a
Tub* is the wallowing of a whale expending its wild, blind
energies on a tub, another is what the physiologists in a
significant secondary use of the word call "teasing." Part
of Swift's humor is to cut and frazzle the reader's nerves by
direct assault; jabber from Irenaus, pseudo-Rosicrucian interpretations, and deliberate obscurities all serve to baffle
and frustrate. Swift teases and irritates his reader, booby
traps him with mock quotations and pretended subtleties,
drops him into yawning chasms in the manuscript, and
alters the character under which he himself writes with
bewildering frequency. Having been provided by an oblig-
ing enemy with a set of annotations, he blandly annotates
the notes and carries out a whole series of mystifying

maneuvers with regard to the publication and authorship of the book. It is as if he were saying, "*I* am the plaything of the whale, passion, which I can divert only by using such foolishness as this—very well; but *you*, the reader, are *my* plaything, too." The tub serves not only to divert but to annoy; and through Swift's many attacks on his reader no doubt involve some directly or indirectly satiric purposes, they also satisfy an impulse to lacerate the reader's feelings, an impulse of which Swift's character is never quite free and which reveals itself overtly in his more scabrous verses.

Within *A Tale of a Tub* one mark of Swift's double attitude is his double use of number and numerology. He mocks the rules of mathematics for their pretended rigor and derides the "mystic" correspondences of numerology; for instance, one of the no less than eleven treatises which his pseudo-author has in hand is a *Panegyrical Essay upon the Number THREE*. The number three, which perverse ingenuity can demonstrate in so many insignificant places, thus signifies for Swift the waste of spirit in brain-maggotry. But *A Tale of a Tub* is itself written to an extraordinary degree in threes. There are, for example, three sons, three varieties of critic, three engines for achieving literary eminence, three characteristics of a critic, three volumes to the proposed treatise on zeal, three distinct anima's or winds to man, three classes of reader—not to mention the three fine ladies, the three tiers to Peter's hat, and the three recommendations as to numerology. Just as *Gulliver* plays with the quirks and oddities of number while satirizing both arithmeticians and numerologists, so *A Tale of a Tub* wavers between derision and fascination; and the only outcome of this equivocation, which can at any time be turned in either direction, is to put the reader in the position of a captive mouse vis-à-vis a triumphant cat.

It is with regard to these latent aggressions against the reader that the significant form of *A Tale of a Tub* comes most directly into question. The story of Peter, Jack, and Martin, which is a satire on religious corruptions, dovetails perfectly well with the digressions, which satirize corruptions in learning. Satire on the Aeolists complements satire on the formalists, and both satires illustrate corruptions in religion and learning. The various prefatory and introductory materials illustrate the empty, pretentious devices of modern authorship; and the ancients-versus-moderns controversy casts a light on the original simplicity and dignity of the institutions which modern folly has corrupted. But the assaults upon the reader surpass or undermine the limits of art; here the author emerges from the frame of his formal presentation to agitate the reader directly. Aesthetically speaking, the effect is kinetic, not to say galvanic—and so, by some strict canons, improper. However this may be, it is certainly divisive. For the reader is not attacked as part of the satire, not lashed for partaking of the errors and follies being mocked in the body of the satiric work. The little tricks and games of esoteric interpretation and numerological obscurity will be puzzling and annoying to a reader almost precisely in the degree that he does *not* partake of "modern" folly. In fact, Swift attacks the reader simply for being the reader; and *A Tale of a Tub* is undoubtedly flawed thereby, as a piece of formal art. But there is at least one variety of art other than formal art, and a spirit so complexly at war with itself as Swift's could find full expression only in that double-dealing which creates a formality chiefly to outrage it.

Houyhnhnm land is of course the *ultima Thule* of Swift's mental voyaging; and even here the savage debacle involves several elements in conflict: witness the animal imagery that Swift applies to the life of reason, the good life. An ironic purpose naturally governs, to a considerable extent, Swift's use of this imagery. As the lack of reason, he implies, will make beasts of men, so the presence of reason will make men of beasts. But the austere rule of reason itself has connotations and overtoes not altogether grateful. The Houyhnhnms are not only superhuman in their repression of the soft emotions, in their reduction of reason to the direct, immediate perception of the unquestionable; they are also inhuman. The usual complaint against Book Four of *Gulliver* is that the satire here fails to be dramatically convincing, that we are not moved by the society of horses to that straightforward love of reason and hatred of unreason which seem to be the author's intent. Houyhnhnm and Yahoo revolt us, if not equally, at least in the same way; they are parodies of the human species, and not all Swift's skill in dramatic presentation can prevent the sledge-drawn horses, with their sober, pseudo-Stoic palavers against passion, from seeming grotesque. One may indeed feel that Swift not only could not but did not want to render the life of reason desirable in its own cold reasonable terms. The life of reason too is a form of assault by Swift on himself and his reader; the sacrifices it demands involve one ultimately in the surrender of humanity itself. Whether or not the author formulated this matter consciously, *Gulliver* implies in its conclusion a despairing suggestion that the life of reason must be lived down as well as up to. The sort of purity which is the norm of Swift's satire, its standard of rest and satisfaction, is not conceivable within a human

frame; either angels or animals are its only conceivable
habitation. That Swift chose animals to embody his conception of the good life suggests that his despair was trembling on the unrecognized verge of hatred. Perhaps this
hatred is the ultimate fate of any man who persists, as long
as Swift did, in manipulating the edged weapons of satire.
But what force urges a man suffering from spiritual hemo-
philia to play so excitedly with edged weapons? It is, I
think, a way of thinking and feeling about human nature
which would prove this nature by the most perilous tests,
which would exalt and liberate it even at the peril of destroying it. The motivation behind this frantic yet stunted
and inverted idealism is perhaps a terror of being used, a
desire to stand free of all the warm, ordinary human en-
tanglements. The passion to test one's human existence by
standing apart from all the comforts that make it human is,
undoubtedly, Quixotic, as its contrary is merely Philistine.
But though it does not provide any comfortable grounds of
practical existence, the austere rage of Swift does mark out
a way of thinking and feeling about one's existence which,
even for those who do not themselves follow it, is strenuous,
perilous, and deeply influential.

For Swift himself the experiment was fatal, as everyone
knows. The narrow isthmus of his arrogant character, a
thin line of shifting sands between the two oceans of personal hysteria and impersonal mechanism, wavered at last
and was overwhelmed. In his final terrible years Swift sat
alone staring at a blank wall and muttering to himself over
and over, "I am what I am. I am what I am."

What was he indeed? What is human character when it
can no longer be distinguished from the socially conditioned reflex on the one hand or the sensually conditioned

impulses of personal hysteria on the other? The form of
Swift's passion was personal and fatal; its content has positive meaning for many—may, indeed, be seen as a constant
preoccupation of the modern conscience. Whether for
social, philosophical, or temperamental reasons or for all
at once, whether from choice or necessity, the exploration
of the most dangerous freedoms of the self (those it wins at
the expense of its own security within any single system of
values) has been taken by a class of modern authors as their
main interest. Whatever discoveries these authors are
found to have made when we consider them as a group,
the fact of their existence and their continuing activity has
been a troubling and significant element in the literary
atmosphere. The relevance of their preoccupations is by no
means diminished today; rather the contrary. Of this author
Swift serves as type and perhaps precursor; and the *Tale of
a Tub*, which raised more monsters from the vasty deep
than ever it diverted, stands at the head of a file of volumes
profoundly expressive of an even more troubled "modern"
spirit than that which the *Tale* seems to take as its most
hated target. Its form is open in several significant ways.
The "story" it starts to tell is never properly concluded,
and even its limited structure as a fable is violated by a
series of deliberate digressions. Its careering, egotistical
author provides, in his intense self-exposure, only the rudi-
ments of a structure. But on the thematic, as well as the
abstract intellectual level, Swift's book lies wide open to a
series of violent, self-destructive antitheses which are the
real heart of its openness. The intensity of its nihilist feeling reminds us of Ibsen and his recurrent suicide fantasies;
the intensity of its dramatic egotism recalls us to the world
of Donne. This vision of the self as splintered but central,

isolated but arrogant, is one in which satire, sinking into the gulf of its own disordered vision, comes to verge on pathology.

Of modern authors, Kafka perhaps comes closest to inhabiting a hall of broken mirrors like Swift's. Although his world is seen, typically, from below the floor rather than from above the horizon, his normal effect is the same: to lacerate, tease, and disquiet the reader. For Swift the human beast is a gibbering baboon, but he looks down on this beast with the calm and lofty eye of a horse; for Kafka the given point of view is that of a dog, a bug, a mouse, an obscure, burrowing, misshapen monster. Both writers use animal imagery to convey their disgust with the human condition; both are expert in the half-serious manipulation of levels of intent and in the use of potential symbolic significances to mask, as well as to reveal, their meaning. Both men stand outside the range of "normal" humanity— the normality is their own conception or misconception, they cannot be sure which—both envy and despise "the others." Both men betray a shuddering horror of domestic intimacy, together with an extraordinary deference before the father-figures of authority; both are extraordinarily nice men with extraordinarily nasty minds. Both are alien and challenging figures, for whom the pure aesthetic effect is a pure aesthetic irrelevance; the sort of freedom in which they are interested is, typically, desperate, frigid, and self-absorbed to the verge of being suicidal. Both employ, as the very structure of their writing, devices of prolonged equivocation; both like to tease the reader with the tricks and traps of numerology.

The central antitheses of Kafka's work are encompassed in the familiar ambiguities of the word "sacred," or, if one prefers anthropological to theological terminology, "taboo." Both words imply among their meanings the notions of "holy" and "accursed," and both meanings are readily convertible. For example, *The Judgment* is a story about Georg Bendemann (literally, "bonds-man") and his guilty feelings of hatred for his father, which make him compulsively obedient to paternal "orders." The protagonist represents Kafka himself, and the diaries work out in detail a correspondence between the two pairs of five-syllable names (Georg-Franz and Bende[mann]-Kafka). Georg Bendemann's hatred for his father is buried, like Franz Kafka's, beneath layers of morbid submissiveness, so that the ending of the book is at once a protest and a form of massive self-punishment. When his father pronounces on Georg the sentence of death by drowning, Georg at once rushes with eager compliance to his own execution; he is hungry for annihilation. As he lets himself drop into the river, we are told in the last sentence of the story that "at this moment an unending stream of traffic was just going over the bridge." Kafka told Max Brod that when he wrote this sentence he "had in mind a violent ejaculation"—and the symbol is fittingly ambiguous as a description of masochistic self-loathing and masochistic self-gratification. But the reader's reaction is one primarily of horror at the judgment which Georg has passed on himself. "Dear parents, I have always loved you, all the same" he calls in a low voice, as he drops; such hidden, yet total self-hatred produces in the reader an instinctive revulsion. Georg is a sacred sacrifice to an evil deity who is, perhaps, no more than his own creation after all.

In the Penal Colony repeats the pattern of abject submission on the part of the actor which generates instinctive

protest in the reader and culminates in total impasse. Here
the level of symbolization is less personal and more ethical.
The penal colony has been ruled by a strict discipline pred-
icated upon a law which permits no doubt of the guilt of
the accused. The central edifice of this legal structure is a
machine that executes wrongdoers by writing the appropriate section of the law, over and over again, with hun-
dreds of slowly deepening needles, on their bodies. Perhaps
there are overtones of masochistic sex in this image; the act
of execution, which places prisoners on a jiggling bed and
writes on their bodies with a complexly moving harrow,
bears some incidental resemblances to sexual intercourse.
But the main emphasis of the symbol is clearly ethical rather
than Freudian. Not even on one who finds it an intensely
painful, "harrowing" experience does sexual intercourse
imprint the motto "Honor thy superiors." There would be
no sense in having the condemned man, who has gone to
sleep on guard, sentenced to sexual intercourse; nor does it
seem in character for him to fear it. On the other hand, the
ethical situation is clear and consistent with Kafka's recurrent view. The old, strict, legalistic ethic, now kept alive
only by a single officer, is being replaced by a milder, more
slovenly and sentimental code. The officer complains that
he can no longer get spare parts for the machine, executions
are not attended as formerly, all the wholesome rigors of
the discipline have fallen into disfavor. Thus the condemned man, instead of going to his death fasting, is now
gorged by the commandant's ladies on candy and vomits
as he assumes the gag. The officer is by no means a repre-
hensible fellow; his ethics are severe but impersonal, and he
is anxious to stand well in the eyes of the explorer. It is,
moreover, a terrible commandment under which he works

and which, when he has violated it, is written into his body —a terrible requirement in two syllables—"Be Just."

Yet for all this, the verdict of the explorer and of the reader can only be unfavorable to the officer and his system of justice. Too much has been made of the gag, the vomit, and the bloody agony which is the price of final illumination. Superficially the story seems to maintain an even, painful balance between slack humanitarianism and inhuman sacramentalism; but, in the final accounting, the reader's sympathies cannot possibly be granted to the officer and his creed. Kafka's theme in this story might be described as the incommensurability of the sacred and the human. But if the merely human is doggy and appetitive, that which is sacred and austere is revolting, and there is no real resolution, except on the simple narrative level. The explorer goes away.

Kafka's equivocation and ambivalence are qualities both persistent and complex; and the duality of his feeling has sometimes been traced to what Swift would call the brain-maggotry of numerological speculation. For instance, Charles Neider has pointed out Kafka's use of the number two as a symbol of community and solidarity; and one might make even more point out of his play with triads, that is, little groups of three, consisting of one leader and two followers. These patterns certainly occur and perhaps have a vague structural or symbolic significance, for instance, in the famous fable of *Metamorphosis*. This is the story, as everyone knows and as the first sentence tells us, of one Gregor Samsa, a commercial traveler, who "awoke one morning from uneasy dreams, and found himself transformed into a gigantic insect." The metamorphosis which so abruptly sets off the story and which animates the hero's

later struggles is a symbolic alienation from humanity. Both
the alienation and the struggles are expressed in combinations of three which either reject Gregor or offer him a
potential status. For instance, his central position in the
family before his metamorphosis is evidenced by the fact
that he then occupied the central one of three bedrooms.
When, after enormous efforts, he emerges from this room
for the first time, he encounters a fully formed and hostile
triad of authorities: the chief clerk, the father, and the
mother confront him directly, two symbols of authority
and discipline, one helpless and unconscious figure of revulsion. Meanwhile in the background appear two symbols
particularly hopeful for Gregor. The maid runs for a lock-
smith, the sister for a doctor; and clearly there is room
within either grouping for a triad including Gregor. But
before help can arrive Gregor has met and been crushed
by the triad of his elders. In fainting, in flight, and in rage
they testify to the utter revulsion which he inspires; and
Gregor is thereby sealed out of the casual, contented fra-
ternity of the well.

That his illness is sexual in nature is suggested by three
clues. A picture of impudent salacity hangs on his wall, and
his only diversion has been to make with a fretsaw a frame
for this pornographic fetish. His erotic memories are either
of failure or of furtive, underhanded success—he recalls
"a chambermaid in one of the rural hotels, a sweet and fleet-
ing memory, a cashier in a milliner's shop whom he had
wooed earnestly but too slowly." His mother refers to an
extraordinary streak of docile domesticity in her son: "he
never goes out in the evenings; he's been here the last eight
evenings and has stayed home every single evening. He
just sits there quietly at the table reading a newspaper or

looking through railway timetables." He has even made a practice of locking his bedroom door at night. All these touches point toward the sort of sexual failure which is typical of the Kafka protagonist—inversion, withdrawal, fetishism, isolation, and untapped sensuality. And this sort of failure is appropriately symbolized by Gregor's isolation from the number three, the masculine number.

(In the esoteric circles where such things are decided, the masculinity of three, as of odd numbers generally, is an ancient and well-disseminated principle. Anthropologists may speculate over its possible reference to the tripartite masculine sex apparatus; for present purposes, it is enough that Kafka might have learned of the association through any of several channels—from Philo Judaeus, from the Kabala, from the Talmud itself, or from a whole string of philosophers, descendants of Pythagoras, not to mention modern ethnologists, folklorists, and students of the occult.)

The use of the triad symbol becomes particularly emphatic when Gregor for the second time comes out of his room to claim a position in the human circle. The occasion of this sortie is the cleaning of his room, an act of double significance since it implies both kindness (the room is described as filthy) and condemnation (to remove Gregor's furniture is to deprive him of the memory as well as the hope of humanity). In open defiance of this change Gregor climbs up the wall to his fetish picture and clings there frantically. Enormous outbursts of rage, terror, and confused revulsion result from this act of insubordination. Gregor, sick with remorse and worry, scuttles out of his room and almost at once comes under attack from his father, who, dressed in the uniform of his work and his au-

Strains of Discord

thority, advances on his insect-son, throwing apples at
him. These weapons, literally so trivial and symbolically
so heavy, crash upon Gregor with the full weight of his
father's once-successful and now-regained sensuality. And
they are terribly reinforced as the mother—revived from
her faint, disheveled, half-disrobed, and followed by her
screaming daughter—rushes out of Gregor's room to reach
"a complete union" with the father. The ruin of Gregor
Samsa is completed by the formation of this triad, which
shuts him out of the very heart of his family. And as his
life slowly ebbs, with the festering of the apple, Gregor
sees constantly before him this pattern to which he is hope-
lessly extraneous, the father flanked by the two women.
Now he sees the triad in moments of weariness and despair,
with his father receiving (as Gregor never had) the help
and support of his wife and daughter. Again he sees it in a
moment of shimmering, shattering, compulsive rage,
brought about by Gregor's own existence:

The father reproached the mother on his right for not having
left the cleaning of Gregor's room to his sister; shrieked at the
sister on his left that never again was she to be allowed to clean
Gregor's room; while the mother tried to pull the father into
his bedroom, since he was beyond himself with agitation; the
sister, shaken with sobs, then beat upon the table with her small
fists; and Gregor hissed loudly with rage because not one of
them thought of shutting the door to spare him such a spectacle and so much noise.

So menacing is the triad of the family that it seems to be
duplicated, if not parodied, in the form of a second triad of
lodgers, who arrive at this point to share the unhappy family's quarters. The lodgers are queer in several ways: they
seem to occupy but one room and to have brought most of

their own furnishings; they are identical in appearance, with full beards, umbrellas, and shabby coats; and they are distinguished only by their position with relation to one another, as the middle lodger, who takes the lead, and the other two, who follow him or repeat what he says.

The nature and function of these lodgers can only be described as puzzling. Their behavior always involves a reversal; their first appearance is just the opposite of their final intent. For example, they are suspicious of the food served them, but soon show satisfaction in it; they wish to hear the sister play on her violin, but are soon bored; learning of Gregor's existence, they threaten the family, but are soon cowed by the father and go off quietly. They are said to have a passion for order and neatness, but it is never conspicuous; and in a moment of acute disgust the middle lodger is capable of spitting on the floor. Most curious of all is their reaction to Gregor's third sortie from his bedroom, in response to his sister's violin playing. They are first amused by the sight of the huge, filthy bug, then angered; then, while the father herds them away from Gregor, the sister slips into the lodgers' room, makes up their beds in a frenzy of activity, and slips out as they disappear into it.

There is a phantom quality to the lodgers, who appear and disappear mysteriously; and the constant unexpected reversal of their intentions may perhaps serve to mock Gregor's (and the family's) undue deference to the triad, which has hitherto been order, community, and strength. They have only to be faced firmly and they disappear; thus, if Gregor in the first episode had only faced the menacing triads down instead of submitting to them, he might have triumphed. The inhumanly rigid law which turns out to be no law at all—at least for the person who supposed it applied to him—is a frequent component of Kafka's writing. As for the sister's curious act of hastily making up their beds, it is an act of deference all the more significant if the authority to which she defers is bogus. She is a key personage with regard to her brother; she is to become his executioner by declaring him out of existence, and in her nubility the family will then find new hope and assurance for the future. She has been Gregor's favorite in the past; even while she is playing the violin, he is dreaming of taking her and keeping her for himself, thus adding incest, that "avarice of the emotions," to his other sexual failings. So that when she undertakes to bring order to the beds of the lodgers, it is an utter apostasy from Gregor. If the authority of the lodgers is genuine, it is a fitting tribute to the principle of masculine authority, in which Gregor is fatally deficient; if their authority is bogus, her tribute can only confirm Gregor's self-abasing belief in it.

Thus the triad principle has undergone a striking reversal in the course of the fable. At first it was a good and healthy principle from which Gregor was tragically alienated, gradually it was modified by the inevitable cruelty and selfishness of the healthy, and at last it appears as a vicious folly. For whether the authority of the lodgers was false in general or only through Gregor's weakness, it is quickly proved false as well as destructive. Confronted by the father with an order to depart, the middle lodger "stood his ground at first quietly, looking at the floor as if his thoughts were taking a new pattern in his head. 'Then let us go, by all means,' he said." And his departure with his two silly, snickering colleagues is clearly the departure of a malignant presence. Indeed, the departure of the malignant triad of lodgers is but a prelude to the loosening of that other malignant triad in which the family has been gripped; and the story ends with the family at leisure, freed from their nightmare by Gregor's death and placidly contemplating a husband for Grete, who will break the whole pattern of triads beyond repair.

The self-lacerating submission already noted in *The Judgment* appears again here; the protagonist approves and relishes his own abolition, as if by this final humility to ingratiate himself with a superior power. The ending of the story thus emphasizes that reading of the fable according to which Gregor, whose only failing was humility, dies in deference to a bogus deity; and on these terms the triads are mere figments of Gregor's sick mind. On the other hand, the incorporation of threes in the structure of the story itself, as well as the logic of Gregor's early situation, suggests another view of the symbolism, scarcely less plausible. Gregor is indubitably sick, his illness is doubtless an alienation, and three is an eloquent symbol of the health and community from which he is isolated. These two interpretations are wholly incompatible; they are also equally cogent. The conflict between them is heightened by Kafka's occasional use of random threes neither to tell his story nor to satirize it but to tantalize the reader. Thus there appear in the story three servants (cook, maid, and char); it is three o'clock in the morning when Gregor dies; the action of the story takes place over a period of three months. Even if one did not know that teasing the reader was a frequent device of Kafka's, one might suspect it from the thick configuration of threes in *Metamorphosis*, their interlocked and layered arrangement, and their occasional complete irrelevance.

Some of the qualities which relate Kafka's mind to Swift's can be seen even in the analysis of these relatively slight pieces; to pursue the parallel through the complex texture of the novels is beyond the scope of this sketch. Yet for all the many congruities of their minds and writings, Kafka is not a satiric author as Swift was—perhaps only because he is not an egotistical one. His bitter, forbidding gaze is directed first against himself; he does not have so much as a platform from which to launch a satiric assault on others. The black pit of his ego is constantly swallowing him up; and though Swift might have said with Archimedes, "Give me a place to stand and I will move the world," Kafka must often have felt that not even the world at the other end of a lever could keep him from collapsing into himself. His use of the open form is that of an ingenious invalid questioning his stupid disease; the deepest reach of his fantastically subtle mind leads only to acceptance of a blind and arbitrary doom. In a sense, he is Swift inverted, Swift cut to pieces by his own outrageously sharp weapons. Kafka, too, has had his William Wottons, who declare from the security of one more or less precarious platform or another that his art is a mere symptom and his meeching submissiveness (like Swift's pathological arrogance) a personal affliction, not an artistic *donnée*. But there is such a thing as being oversolicitous of the reader's mental security. Within a culture which is itself reasonably secure there will always be a place for works which consciously test the reader's self-definition. Conceivably one could postulate a level at which such works are formed not around the intent of the author but around the resistance of the reader. The sense of this level is, I think, one peculiar quality common to both Swift and Kafka. They are strict and strenuous authors in reading whom one can get badly hurt. Yet there is always a sense of adventure. At their best they yield an intense and painful hilarity, a vision of suffocating, crawling conformity lightning-lit by the blinding perspectives of dread.

∽ VIII ∽

Romantic Openness and the Unconscious

NOTHING is more frequent, in this topic, than the only apparent contrary. When the mind turns the sharp edge of its satiric disapproval against its own nature, we get an openness which in its austerity, compression, and self-limitation seems classical. Such openness seems to be the opposite, but is really the complement, of romantic openness, in which the mind strains to remain unresolved before the fullness or magnitude of an experience and will not close form because to do so implies exclusion. Both patterns involve and express a sort of humiliation of the mind, which, since it is always in art presumed a free agent, must inevitably appear to wish its own defeat, hence to be perverse. Yet it is often anguished as well, and its action involves not only a testing but ultimately a negation of individual identity; the purpose behind this depressing sequence is only sometimes exemplary. Annihilation, as we know, may be sought for its own sake.

In the early days of romanticism failure to complete a literary form was quite freely accepted and sometimes proclaimed as an evidence of largeness of mind and total receptivity to experience. Scornful of the narrowly boxed cosmos created out of Newton's three laws of motion and of the strict literary forms which seemed to accompany and express it, the romanticist indulged his soul in immense cloudy visions or searches, the common psychological character of which was to stretch and measure the ego against the vastness of an infinite universe. For a critic like J. G. Herder all formal literary unity was an artificial, unnatural, constraining concept which he could neither endorse nor try to exemplify. For a writer like Novalis the search after total experience was so absorbing that it could only be represented as a lifelong self-destructive search after an unknown and probably unknowable value symbolized, vaguely enough, as a "blue flower." Trying to define this objective rather more distinctly than Novalis could bring himself to do, modern critics have been led to think of the *Ding an sich*. Novalis himself was led to a desire for death so acute that it has made him almost a paradigm of the unhappy, intense romanticist whose yearning for ideal beauty drives him to an early grave. A sequence of melancholy young men followed in his path, as he pursued that of his hero, Heinrich von Osterdingen. What Heinrich was to Novalis, Alastor was to Shelley, Endymion to Keats, and Juan to Byron. The story of the search for unearthly beauty and its melancholy conclusion culminates fittingly in the weird immolation of Baker by Boojum in "The Hunting of the Snark."

All these fables are open in the vague sense that the hero is driven by an impulse he can never make clear toward a state which seems to transcend the human condition. Sometimes he cannot find what he is looking for, sometimes it recedes as he approaches, so that the search becomes endless, and the form is apt to be open terminally. Sometimes the hero successfully transcends the human condition and seizes his *summum bonum* but finds that it exhausts his already deplenished energies; thus he dies immediately upon fruition, like a male salmon. This is internal two-way openness, such as we have noted in Keats, can recall in Wagner, and will see raised to something like a theatrical principle in *Axel's Castle*. Or finally one has the different variants of the Faust figure, who try to encompass all experience at once, straining their energies against the sheer limitations of personal identity and the capacities of human speech—till they either burst like Aesop's frog or give up the effort to communicate altogether. Thus Mynheer Peeperkorn, the incoherent Dutch invalid of *The Magic Mountain*, outdoes the most vociferous of the talkers who populate this talkative book simply by dwelling with a profound relish, which is above all grammar and beyond all coherent assertion, on such good, simple things as bread, gin, and nature. By saying nothing, he implies the vital reverence which is everything. A gesture, a meaningless phrase, a touch, an inaudible dedication—it is all in the refusal to smudge what is sacred with mere words—and the chord unfulfilled, the beat missed, by a familiar inversion, becomes supremely emphatic.

Other pieces of writing that try to say nothing less than everything fall back on different forms of openness. *Finnegans Wake* is a perfectly closed cycle in one obvious sense, since, after four books of the universal dream which takes us from unity to duality to multiplicity and back to unity, the last half of the last sentence fits into the first half of the first one and starts us around the cycle again. But the infinite variety of epicycles, language levels, and punning allusions leaves the book, as it were, laterally open. Its vision is apocalyptic and synoptic; there is nothing which cannot be brought within its web, and as it assumes a pattern of total relevance, no conceivable choice or combination of implications can be rejected from the pattern, or omitted. Perhaps it will not sound merely plaintive if one says that *Finnegans Wake* is harder to read than it can possibly have been to write. In both cases whatever comes to hand is all right; but in such a quadriliberal pussycorner of attractable racticulations it is easier to take any direction than to follow a particular one.

Ever since the first edition of *Leaves of Grass* American writing has included a strain of enthusiastic, receptive, indeterminate openness to experience which finds expression in loose, unstructured form. Literary criticism has tried, lately, to find wit, point, and deliberate structure in the poems of Whitman; the attempt may not be altogether futile, but if fully successful it will surely cut a cubit from Whitman's stature. The comic, elusive, exuberant movement of *Song of Myself* is not only unbounded by structural formalities, but scornful of them. Perhaps the supreme impression conveyed by the poem is elasticity; it is willing to overstep any boundaries, confident of its own ability to exist, completely unstructured, as raw sentiment or perception. The poem is simply the theater of a struggle between the infinite ego and the innumerable thing. By increasing subtlety, by triumphant versatility, by an audacious leveling movement, the poet's ego converts the whole world to its aliment. One is reminded of E. E. Cummings' reputed remark to a lady who reproached him with exaggerating his own small significance in the cosmos. "After all," she declared, "you are only a small part of the world." "On the

contrary," said he, "the world is only a small part of me."
The joke behind much of Whitman's poetry is that, however the world swells and expands, it always finds Walt
Whitman is just a little bit bigger. In their diverse ways,
lesser figures like Cummings and William Saroyan carry on
this free, frank, open tradition, which at its best does not
even pause to impress the bourgeois but plunges after the
big feeling, the direct approach, the complete commitment,
as if it were a test of one's very existence.

It is a curious social phenomenon on other levels—I think
it is a good deal less interesting—that loudly discontented
young men should be making a noise for themselves, at the
same time and through substantially the same channels, in
London and San Francisco. Most of the angry young novels
pothering around Great Britain these days seem to concern plebeian young men who, in a straightforward way,
want large motor cars, large incomes, and receptive young
ladies. The novels recount how, in various bounderish
ways, the young men achieve these ends; they tend, thus, to
be straightforward, literal-minded exterior novels of social
mobility rather like the early novels of H. G. Wells. But the
play which has made, to some extent, the reputation of the
London group is a play about an unstructured young man
who, having put himself in surroundings at once dreary and
peculiar, seems to expect them to rise above him. Since he
does almost no thinking about his circumstances but merely
reacts to them with the bellow of a stricken animal, an
audience is naturally impelled to speculate on what ails
him. Jimmy Porter is clearly delighted to find himself the
subject of anxious concern by the characters of the play
and by the paying audience; indeed, the desire to occupy
this position seems, to at least one unsympathetic viewer, to

be what chiefly ails him. It is truly a humane age which will stop to inquire so anxiously after the meaning of such prolonged and repeated yelps of unlocalized disquiet.

Probably the last word in the literature of total experience is that written by Mr. Jack Kerouac, in a recent novel *On the Road*. The hero is a mixed-up bopster for whom every experience must be at its most intense all the time. He has women on the east coast and on the west coast and can never settle with any one of them because he is so sensitive to the demands of the others. Thus he spends his time, literally, on the road, with various companions to whom he is also sensitive. In an insane, delirious parody of the analytic situation, he sits down with a friend to analyze every last implication of a conversation; and as the implications of the analytic statements become tangled with the implications of the original discussion, the characters manage to reduce themselves to absolute speechlessness. Indeed, the hero, having passed through various stages of incoherence, finally achieves the acme of sensation, and complete inability to talk at all. He simply drives automobiles about, furiously, as if in some sort of insane rage to catch up with everything; this he calls "feeling time." Open to all experiences and quite incapable of deciding among them, suffering, intense, and incurably self-conscious, he is a model of the modern man of sensibility.

There may be stages of unstructured, raw sentiment beyond Kerouac; but it will take a good man to discover and exploit them. Meanwhile, one may be momentarily entertained to note the possibilities of total silence and uncreated works of art as a kind of mocking ultimate for a certain sort of sensibility. Some critics have said in all seriousness that the last and supreme work of Rimbaud was the final eighteen years of silence by which he implied that every-thing, absolutely everything, had already been said. This is openness with a vengeance—a sort of absurdity, perhaps, but with the insidious possibility of being a sublime one. Melville is another case in point. Ibsen exploited these ironic possibilities in the figure of Ulric Brendel, who, amid the stolid representative characters of *Rosmersholm*, has the free spirit of a wealthy bankrupt; he has only dreams, but he has never spoilt or spent them by giving them a specific shape and definite character.

Ibsen took an ironic view of Ulric Brendel (who is a caricature of Hialmar Ekdal, who is a caricature of Peer Gynt, who . . .), and it is hard to avoid this stance in dis-cussing creators who are so creative that they scorn the humble craft of actually creating something. The king's new clothes were less chimerical than creativity of this exalted character. But a modern tendency which has been more solemnly received is that of creating the impression of passionate profundity by means of willful omissions, con-scious disarrangements, and deliberate refusals to resolve clear logical or grammatical conflicts. By devices of this sort, the author involves the reader in the actual work of construction, teasing him by holding forth several alternate ways to resolve a particular pattern of conflict, and yet holding back authorial sanction for any. We have noted that some of the poems of Dylan Thomas are grammat-ically inconsequent, impossibly punctuated, and discordant in their images beyond the possibility of either visualization or comprehension. There seems no reason to doubt that some at least of this disorganization was deliberate, that it aimed at creating discord and difficulty, partly for expres-sive purposes, partly for their own sake.

We tread here on the toes of the literary hierophant, but still it seems worth saying that one of the generic functions of incomprehensibility in modern writing is the titillation of the reader's curiosity. Juxtapositions which seem too significant or too revelatory are often withheld: for instance, *The Waste Land* would have been, in many respects, a much clearer poem if Eliot had carried out his original intent of incorporating "Gerontion" and omitting "Phlebas the Phoenician." On a smaller scale, grammatical forms are sometimes deliberately made incongruous with logical relations; a particular variety of this device is the "because" phrase which states not a causal relation but a co-ordinate fact or even a result. One also notes the logical alternative that is deliberately blurred, confused, and even identified with its antithesis. Devices of this sort are frequent in the poetry of Auden. Still another device of evocatory obscurantism is the purely private reference or association of ideas, in which the difficulty of making a connection outweighs or obscures entirely the significance of any possible connection which is discovered. Deepening obscurity, which is perfectly legitimate, may shade into absolute unintelligibility and hocus-pocus, which is not, without losing its power to provoke speculation. Thus the white bear that quoted Virgil in the fifth sonnet of Thomas' sequence does not really function as a literary reference; if one doesn't know where such a bear appears in literature or what he connotes or what passage of Virgil he is likely to be reciting (either *Aeneid* VI or "Eclogue IV," one guesses, but only because they are the mantic areas), the passage has produced exactly its intended effect. And if one does not know what is the subject of the verb "cross-hatched" in the last lines of the same sonnet, or whether "pin-legged"

modifies "angel" or "Adam," or how the last line is gram-
matically connected with anything at all, these darknesses
too are but part of the total discord and obscurity which is
Thomas' chosen effect.

Finally, apart from all these more or less expressive aims,
there is absolute irrational obscurity of the provocatory
sort exemplified in the *mondo* and *koan* of Zen Buddhism,
which by placing ideas and objects in absurd relations to
one another aim to carry out violent dislocation of conventional categories and thus free the mind to grasp the inner
thinginess of the particular thing and ultimately the all-
thinginess of all-things. One explodes the familiar mode of
vision by placing intolerable strains upon it. Whatever new
vision rises out of this experience (as with the *Angst* and
"leap" of existentialism, only the preliminary dilemma is
structured; the conclusion is almost wholly undetermined)
will presumably be deeper than, or at least different from,
that which was destroyed. The prevalence and widespread
popularity of these extreme intellectual trapeze tricks may
be attributed to the wide dissemination of a conversion
psychology without a controlling intellectual structure.
What sort of kicks one can get from a conversion *voulu* I
do not know and do not want to imagine; but the change is
symptomatic of a broad degeneration in the theme of the
search, which is now properly motivated by the sticks of
absurdity and anxiety rather than the carrot of faith.

A key figure in modern romantic openness is probably
D. H. Lawrence. The fact that he worshipped the dark,
irrational forces of blood and bowels, despising rationality
as such, suggests one reason for his scorn of the form too
narrowly closed; but the curious circumstance is that this
did not lead him by any means to create shapeless rhap-

sodies. There is an odd streak of John Bunyan in Lawrence; a good many of his characters are simply versions, in modern dress, of Mr. Badman. He is a lay preacher, then, of considerable power; alternately, he is an eloquent writer of incantatory prose. But the structure of his novels is not, ordinarily, open to any notable degree. The narrative may be, and usually is, fairly primitive; but it achieves the modicum of resolution normal in the modern novel. Its episodes may be loosely joined or altogether unconnected on the level of mechanical causation but are usually broadly linked in terms of someone's psychological development. And in fact it is in their concept of character that Lawrence's novels are most interestingly open. Fluid, violent, demanding, inconsistent, and direct, the characters of Lawrence have a vitality which refuses to be fixed; their sense of life as pattern is weak, their sense of impulse and need very strong. In the rituals of private religion they achieve various provisional and temporary fulfillments; but beyond and beneath all forms their allegiance is to something fluid and impermanent, so that, unless they are mere allegorical abstractions, one never feels them capable of, or interested in, any sort of settlement with life. There is a level of existence beneath ideas and institutions, beyond thought and speech and literature itself, after which they are always groping. They proclaim an inward grace of which no adequate outer sign really exists and which Lawrence can suggest only by their flaring, nervous, irritable speech. The chief quality of his characters is their sensitivity or lack of sensitivity to a set of mysterious interior variables; the chief quality which the novels themselves cultivate is sensitivity and intensity of response.

In itself, this cultivation of intensity or sensitivity for its own sake is not a form of, or even an index to, literary openness; indeed, one may sense that a tight structure and close parallels might serve the ends of the intense writer even better than a diffuse or unresolved form. But the turbulent subconscious, in which Lawrence seeks a deep, restless peace, may easily be transformed into a fractured and divided subconscious, rebellious, tormented, and guilty. Here one is involved at once in various forms of openness.

This is the special quality of William Faulkner's vision. Immersed in waves of violent, contradictory sensation, his characters barely emerge from the swirl of passion long enough to articulate that existence is meaningless and incommunicable. *The Sound and the Fury* is the supreme achievement of the canon largely because it does succeed in making this assertion more or less unequivocally. Elaborately patterned and complexly disorganized in temporal sequence, the novel seems at one point to reach a climax in the declaration of Christian religious values. "Dilsey's day" is Easter Sunday, and at the church she attends with the sacred idiot Benjy the miracle of resurrection is exuberantly, almost incoherently, proclaimed. Yet, after all, it is a Negro's miracle, in the context of a Negro religion; and how it applies to white folks, specifically Compsons, is far from clear. The final picture we are left with is of Jason frantically whipping old Queenie round the statue on the left-hand side, because it is only the left-hand side which is familiar—"orderly"—to Benjy. "Order" of this sort will stop an idiot's bawling; but by the rest of us, and presumably this includes the author, it must be somewhat sardonically viewed. Faulkner's novel, though it not only includes but is patterned around the Christian order of time and value, also includes a powerful and bitterly nihilistic negation of that and all other schemes of order. A bitter analogy is found in the conclusion of *As I Lay Dying*, where the one Bundren with elements of unclouded vision is finally carted off to the insane asylum at Jackson.

Order is possible, but not for the characters central to the novel; it is necessary but intolerable, private and therefore disorderly. Within *The Sound and the Fury* both complexes of attitude are shown as ultimate in terms of human circumstances. Dilsey's reconciliation to the Christian virtues of patience and humility is inconceivable to Jason though inevitable to her; Jason's exasperations with the very structure of the universe are inconceivable to Dilsey though inevitable to him. Both these resolutions are perfectly adequate to round off the experience of the individual character (Benjy's world is merely Jason's chaos heightened to idiocy and deadened by imperception; Quentin's world is merely Dilsey's without the hope of personal salvation). But the two of them juxtaposed suffer from the disadvantage of a flat contradiction. Their effect is at once violent, conclusive, and discordant.

It is not only that the "ideology" of Faulkner's novel is a matter of conflicting and unreconciled opposition or that the reader's sympathies are held in permanent suspense and unreleased tension. As my colleague Walter Slatoff has made brilliantly clear,[1] the very style is built around a grammatical counterpart of open form—the oxymoron, or flat opposition of modifiers and word modified. Whether one thinks it a mere trick of style or an integral expression of Faulkner's own vision, this rhetorical figure is overwhelmingly frequent in Faulkner's work, wher-

---

[1] "The Edge of Order: the Pattern of Faulkner's Rhetoric," *Twentieth Century Literature* (October, 1957), pp. 107–127.

ever the author speaks in his own person. On each page one finds expressions like "musclebound eagerness," "a soundless alacrity," "a thick, light voice," and "a prolonged and suspended fall" (this collection is from the first few pages of Dilsey's day, in *The Sound and the Fury;* a culling of the later novels would multiply it a thousandfold).

When it is not a mere clattering of metaphorical pots and pans, a device like this serves to create an immense sense of furious, blind energy up against a blank wall—a moving and appropriate emotional climate for a story of decadence and deterioration. Within its inherent limitations the conflict of irresistible force and immovable object represents a literary theme like others; and its fulfillment accounts, on at least one view, for the often paralyzing force and power of Faulkner's art. The author himself, on the other hand, seems never to have been fully satisfied with this definition of his form, his theme, or his talent; and, indeed, on the cosmic level the enraged impasse does yield a rather limited view of things, while on the literary level it leads to a style at once inflated, bombastic, and inflexible. Stylistically, however, Faulkner has no characteristic alternative mode; and structurally, gains in clarity seem to be made only at the cost of an immense drop in literary energy. Of recent years he has taken to expounding with increasing solemnity, verbosity, and pedantry a symbolical-allegorical version of Christian doctrine quite unrelated to the devastating Schopenhauer pessimisms of Jason Compson III. There is no question of his ability to round out and close off this Christian fable, which carries within itself its own set of ultimate symbols. But to make this symbolic material intimate to the human substance of a novel and significant in terms of it (rather than the facile contrary), is a problem that he has, so far, not solved. Increasingly, the symbolic material seems to exist inertly, as an abstract and solemn scheme imposed on subject matter of steadily diminishing vitality.

Not only does the solemn expository symbolism which is easily closed off militate to some degree against the ferocious logical confusion, the wild, incantatory self-bewilderment which is Faulkner's most moving manner, it is also ill-related to that curious critical credo (its multiple illogicalities are neatly outlined by Mr. Slatoff) which makes the magnitude and magnificence of his fall the chief criterion of an artist's success and which underwrote Faulkner's early endeavors to say, in his novels, The Whole Thing. Without endorsing fully this super-romantic credo, which converts the artist into a frenzied heaven stormer, one may still feel that the blazing, meaningless melodrama of his early works is preferable to the torpid symbol-shifting of his later ones. The taut and living speech of *The Sound and the Fury* is its own, and the novel's, full justification.

But, leaving this question aside for the moment, Faulkner's novel is one more token that total impasse and complete irresolution can become the center of a work which gives at least the appearance of being in the closed form; and such a work may be imbued with tension and pervasive energy while a work which is technically in the open form remains diffuse and languid. The problem of openness or closedness of form is a matter akin to but essentially distinct from the general question of the texture of a literary work, the tightness or slackness of its detailed patterning. Perhaps the only definition of relation which can be proposed is a negative one. Since the closed form is familiar

and anticipated and easy to suggest, even with apparently
intractable materials, there is likely to be a particular impetus behind any work that asserts irresolution and openness as a principle of its organization.

Somewhat apart from Faulkner's Promethean efforts at
all-inclusiveness are the relatively fragile and sensitive mo-
tions by which Virginia Woolf, attempting to penetrate
and synthesize the evanescent mystery of several points of
view, was forced to conclude in romantic metaphysical
irresolution. *To the Lighthouse* is clearly concerned, in a
major way, with the difficulties of communication. Mr.
Ramsay's exhausting raids into the outer spaces of metaphysics are but one aspect of his cataclysmic failure to
communicate with his family and the outside world in
general. The very method of the novel, where long interior monologues are interspersed with desultory action,
seems intended to show us how much of human consciousness lies beneath the surface and never attains overt expression. And in the course of the action itself efforts to
communicate are brought, one after another, to the edge
of inevitable failure. Although she pulls things together
at the dinner party, Mrs. Ramsay sees that they immediately
fall apart: William Bankes never does get to say how beautiful Mrs. Ramsay is, nor for that matter does Charles Tans-
ley; James's rage against his father finds no expression;
Lily Briscoe's picture is never painted; the expedition to
the lighthouse is deferred; the fisherman's boy callously
cuts a slab off a fish and flings the body, still living, back
into the sea; and the solitary epitaph of all dead hopes is
murmured by Mr. Ramsay in the despairing lines of
Cowper,

> But I beneath a rougher sea
> Was whelmed in deeper gulfs than he.

Yet in the final scene an effort is made to redeem all these failures. The surviving Ramsays do reach the lighthouse, though the experience seems in some ways disappointing; Mr. Ramsay manages to say, painfully, two kind words to his son James; and his daughter manages to see him, briefly, in a fresh and favorable light. Simultaneously, Lily Briscoe, painting painfully away on the shore, manages to finish her picture. At least some and perhaps all of these incidents are probably intended as a symbolic rounding-off of the novel. Someone has made contact with someone or something else; the striving for communication-expression has born some fruit. But quite apart from the obscurities of symbolism, which are many, the difficulty must be sensed that these final episodes of *To the Lighthouse* are only thinly related to previous ones. Time passes, the wind shifts, and the Ramsays go to the lighthouse; it is as undramatic as that. Even Lily Briscoe's picture is completed, not as a result of a sustained effort, but by a sudden, unpremeditated stroke, a straight line in the middle of it. Perhaps these facts, in their totality, express an insight—that it is only in rare and lucky moments that understanding and communication are achieved, almost without our active seeking of them. But this insight, however valid in itself, will scarcely justify the climactic emphasis which seems to be laid on Mr. Ramsay's arrival at the lighthouse and Lily's completion of her picture. If communication really is random, then how meretricious to suggest that it is climactic. Mrs. Woolf's novel wavers rather unhappily between an arbitrary and a frankly irresolute ending; and, ultimately, it leaves us with a sense that the jump has not been cleanly taken. If communication is so difficult that Mrs. Woolf cannot even communicate clearly to us whether or not it has taken place, her novel must be judged a symptom, not a triumph.

A great deal of modern literary communication takes place through what we know, or have been told we know, about the subconscious. The doctrine of the collective or intracultural subconscious, in any of its several manifestations, is a great device for cementing, not only one symbol to another, but one literary work to another, one myth or archetype to every other myth or archetype. This is the synoptic vision with a vengeance. Yet on any less exalted basis the subconscious is more apt to be a solvent than a glue. Upon an awareness of it depends the whole metaphysics of ambiguity, which reaches such a pitch of contrivance in novelists like Gide, Faulkner, and Mrs. Woolf that even statements about ambiguity must be ambiguously phrased and rational discourse degenerates into analysis of analytic phrases about analytic phrases. If there is a distinction to be made, it must be that Faulkner is in the immediate Lawrence mode of enraged omphalos-intuition, which is ultimately nonconformist and Calvinist in its tonalities, while Mrs. Woolf and Gide relate to an ironic and secular tradition of self-puzzlement, in which the self is a quizzical set of disparate incompatibles, rather than wiredrawn, vibrant unity. Lawrence and Faulkner stand at the end of a long line of heroic creators of literary heroism; they magnify the extraordinary capacity for doing or suffering and exemplify, themselves, the St. Sebastian stance which is ultimate for this kind of thing. And, indeed, one may sense a kind of grandeur, available through non-logical or anti-logical feeling, which rationality with its sterile, skeptical insights can hardly rival. This is an ultimate aspect of that "dissociation of thought and feeling" noted by Eliot in the writers of the nineteenth century. Faulkner in his shaman personality not only does not think, he actually could not, since most of his feeling—and that of his characters—is directed immediately and violently against logical categories. Thus the last resort of romantic affirmation seems sometimes to be a willful burrowing into the dark anonymous mysteries of feeling, where, in peace or anguish, the final elements of individuality expire.

Anonymity the last refuge of identity—it is one of those paradoxes of which, increasingly these days, the cosmos seems to be inherently composed but about which, by the very act of adopting the framework of rational discourse, one is precluded from saying anything. It is a passing point of interest, of course, that the open form seems well adapted to expressing man's position in an outsize universe or a divided and fragmentary one. But openness relates also to several concepts of the self, which may be conceived as pervading the cosmos, indistinguishable from it, and thus infinite, or as being an endless indecisive battle-field of impulses, concerning which even the statement that they are contradictory is subject to contradiction. It is the supreme romanticism to try, as Faulkner tries, to combine the infinitely extended with the infinitely fractured view of mental experience. In this undertaking the very categories of judgment are muddled into a critical *credo quia absurdum,* and empty grandiloquence is judged to have aimed highest because it has fallen flattest. On this plane the real, opposed, but non-contradictory impulses of emphatic tension are in danger of being transmuted into a logical contradiction that amounts to nothing more than air articulated into nonsense.

The solemn practical joke has a role in modern writing not easy to assess; for the joke itself may be only the reverse side of a "serious" construct and may, in addition to being a joke, have its own provocative or otherwise intentional aspects. Nonsense writings are no longer just nonsense, but concealed acts of aggression or appeasement; only general literary solemnity prevents us from saying that the actual effect of much "serious" writing includes that of a hoax. For example, it is a frequent device in modern writing to choose as the observer and recounter of a story someone who cannot possibly understand it: an infant, an idiot, an outsider, or a dog. If one makes the events incomprehensible to the observer for no such evident reason but simply because he declines to ask one or two practical, matter-of-fact questions, one has achieved pretty much the pattern of a Henry James story. Much of James's fiction involves a series of games and inferences by which a complex confusion of half-meanings and guesses is accumulated around a void which—for all one can tell—might be filled by a perfectly simple, natural statement of fact. It was not simply self-deprecation which led him to refer to a novel like *The Sacred Fount* as "a consistent joke"; the novel has indeed the quality of being built like a riddle. It is a tissue of hazards and analogies probing a heart of darkness which may itself be willful—the overflow of a deeper darkness in the heart of a narrator, from whom the very tissue of the novel has been spun. The novel is, thus, or may be, simply a joke, since it may turn out to be about nothing but the mind in which such fantastic suspicions could form and grow into so vast a submarine structure without one least particle of outside evidence. If it is not a parody of the author himself, it is or may be a burlesque of the narrator; and the line between narrator and author is, shall we say, incautiously thin.

Far less obscure is the joke element in an author like Gertrude Stein. The fallacy of imitative form is nicely illustrated by her belief that monotonous, cyclical life is best represented in monotonous, cyclical writing. Letting the language take its own direction, without the interfering and controlling hand of the artist results in little association and pattern clusters:

> They cannot.
> A note
> They cannot
> A float.
> They cannot.
> They dote.
> They cannot.
> They as denote.

And finally these little agrammatical word-gyrations give way to direct burlesques and parodies of accepted structures; Act III begins over again in the middle of Act III, and the confusion spreads outward through the bewildered characters to the indulgent audience. "It is seldom," says an interpreter, "that Miss Stein's tongue is not in her cheek"; one of the greatest jokes is, apparently, the lurking possibility that anything which seems "serious" may really be a joke and vice versa. This is a type of structural openness not very far removed from buffoonery. Beyond it lies only a variety of writing unstructured to the point of perfect meaninglessness—black marks arbitrarily collocated on paper, from which the creator has withheld or withdrawn his own sense of order, so that the reader may be free to discover-create-attribute his own. Literature as Rorschach test is an ultimate in romantic egotism; it reduces every work of art to the reflection of one's own features. It is not even deep calling to deep, but surface to surface, Narcissus in two dimensions.

∽ IX ∾

Some Aesthetic Adjustments

KNOWING simply that it is very common may calm some terrors about the open form. With a quick eye, a keen nose, and a mediocre amount of determination, the critic who wants to do so can easily discover an element of openness in almost any literary form. If it is not an ideological or emotional issue left unresolved, it may well be a narrative thread left untied, a sequence of images unlinked to other sequences, or a narrative framework casually overstepped by authorial comment. That these elements are insignificant provides no sure recourse from critical inquisitions. Once alerted to the concept of ambivalence (which is, on a small scale, very much what openness is on a large one), what incredible trophies have not the devoted critics produced! One naturally hesitates to propose another such game of hare and hounds—especially when the hare is, once again, an exceedingly ill-defined animal.

Nothing is easier than to raise the standard of closed form so high that it becomes quite meaningless. Thus one discovers openness where the author did not intend it and could not avoid it, where the work itself has nothing to gain by its existence. Given the fallen state of human nature, works of art can scarcely be expected to find final resolution of all the problems—intellectual, social, psychological, and artistic—with which they deal. Perhaps in a state of society where a public philosophy prevails, providing correct and ultimate answers to all major questions, literary forms may without effort approximate complete closedness. Dante's Florence and Stalin's Russia are examples of such societies—societies necessarily provincial, but where authors were supplied with ready-made universal systems of general value, into which it was relatively easy to fit and from which it was relatively hard to escape. Under these circumstances a work of art which fails to resolve its major issues must (unless these issues are very esoteric indeed) be thought to avoid resolution deliberately. In our own hit-or-miss, cosmopolitan culture, on the other hand, few works can avoid remaining, or seeming to remain, open, in one particular or another, from one aspect or another.

Yet primary emphasis in this, as in all formal matters, must be on the autonomy of the artist. No matter how tightly closed the philosophy of his own day may be, no matter how intimately he adheres to it, his work may take advantage in various ways of the open form. And the converse point also obtains; a sort of closed effect is always available to any artist who chooses to make use of it. No experience is, of its own nature, unstructurable; no literary mode is too refractory; and no artist is so barren of resource against the raw materials of his experience that he cannot scratch up the appearance of a resolution if he feels that his artistic advantage will be served by doing so. In point of fact, the very definition with which we started presumed a measure of deliberate but not arch or perverse purpose as the condition of the category.

On the whole, it has not proved difficult to find examples of open-structured work from the areas of poetry, prose fiction, and the drama; and while these examples have sometimes tended to verge on the unnatural and deliberately contrary-minded, there are evidently several areas where the open form serves expressive or constructive purposes.

In Ibsen, Keats, Flaubert, and Tennessee Williams one observes an ethical-aesthetic ("real life"–"imagination") contrast which is treated in vindictive, crushing, self-tormenting terms. There are variations here—the first two are given to calling attention to the aesthetic delusion as the second pair are not—but the culmination of all four patterns is in something remarkably close to the death wish; this may very well be conceived as a larger perversity with which the lesser perversity of open form coincides, but from another aspect it gives the form an expressive content which is almost uniquely appropriate.

A second grouping, of Shakespeare, Cervantes, Stendhal, and Gide, seems to make use of open form for lighter purposes—sometimes for comedy, more often for ironic inconclusiveness, and occasionally for a deeply recessed mirror vision in which the work of art itself occupies the foreground of its own picture. Many of the works in this class imply a hierarchical view of the world and play in a detached way with the different outlooks implicit in different positions within the hierarchy. In Stendhal and Gide we get something close to masquerading for its own sake or for the sake of the possible melodramatic effects. And from the aspect of tonality it is perhaps true that Mrs. Woolf belongs in this grouping rather than in that of the furious confused introspectors with whom her indecisiveness about indecision itself finally aligned her.

In a third provisional group fall those poets whose dramatic display, intellectual energy, and stylistic floridity give to their "metaphysical" manner an aspect significantly "open." Donne and Eliot use difficult metaphors strategically, and some of Eliot's are so difficult as to be, on a direct level, impossible; but dramatically they are easily resolved, like those of Donne himself. Aside from the dramatic metaphysical style of Donne and Eliot, Herbert exemplifies a quiet manner, Auden a restless one; these individual and temperamental colorations suggest the wonderful fullness with which metaphysical energy can infuse symbols when it is fully centered on something, and the diffuseness to which, simply as a manner, it is liable. But that athletic metaphysical verse is more than a mannerism, that it may serve to create a kind of baroque structure the energy and audacity of which remove it entirely from the criterion of good and bad taste, is exemplified in Crashaw and (to some degree) in Dylan Thomas. This athletic dilemma gives a special complexity to the whole topic of metaphysical verse, on which I am very far from thinking the last word has been said.

The two last groups of writers using open form are less separate "groups" than extreme examples of earlier attitudes. The satiric vision of Swift and Kafka is sharpened and inverted to the point where it results substantially in the destruction of both the satire and the satirist. Within the satiric mode this is essentially the divided vision of a writer like Ibsen. It is important and interesting that both Ibsen and Kafka are under the primary influence of Kierkegaard; the natural affinities of open-formed writing with the aesthetic-ethical-religious trichotomy simply confirm its capacity for stating a central concern with the self. (On the other hand, Ibsen's emotional tone is lofty and satiric like that of Swift; Kafka's is self-despising and masochistic like that often found in Flaubert.) In Lawrence and Faulkner the romantic desire to measure one's ego against the measureless cosmos is ballooned into blind, subconscious gigantism.

To these provisional and clearly makeshift categories one might add many examples of open-formed work where the problem of function and motivation has remained more or less indistinct. In the background of Molière's *Misanthrope*, for example, we discern a philosophic and social impasse which has brought many men up against a blank wall. What does the just man do when he finds himself alone in a psychotic society? Whatever he does, is he funny or tragic when he does it? The deviant as silly or as an agent of divine enlightenment represents an alternative deeply fixed in the human condition; and ultimately it must have raised in Molière's mind a question of self-definition before the implications of which he drew back. His comedy is more than a comedy, though it is a culmination of the sort of comedy he began writing in *Les Précieuses ridicules* and brought to a first climax in *Tartufe;* the most one can say of it is that it brings us with brilliant force to a recognition of impasse and incompatibility by existing within our minds as two plays at once. There is no way to stop Alceste from looking foolish and Célimene from looking charming; there is no way to stop Alceste from looking honorable and Oronte from looking despicable; when Célimène refuses to forego a society composed of Orontes, the play arrives at two emotionally incompatible qualities —and then simply stops. With it stop all sorts of developments in Molière's career; among all the other possibilities there remains the depressing one that he simply could not make up his mind about what he had done. Impasse itself may of course be a discovery; if the ultimate fool is something of a hero (and vice versa), this tells us something about the categories "fool" and "hero." But the play itself is not transcendent; it is simply open. Any transcendence we see is our own. Openness is used to reveal a contrast and then to shut off its development. Why a man crawls out on a logical limb like this and then saws it off is obviously a question with a lot of answers; but that the open form somehow helps him to express his feelings about the process is apparent. On the other hand, *The Cherry Orchard*, without bringing its characters up against any such philosophic ultimates, manages to remain indecisive about whether they are pathetic or ridiculous and so builds its main effects, as it is usually played, on the indecisive mingling of emotional elements. Finally, the vaudeville of plays which concern the creation of the play being watched (like Cummings' *Him* or Pirandello's *Six Characters*) and the scheme of the novel that describes the process of its own creation (this is familiar in Gide and Huxley) are continuing examples of openness used to gain perspective.

Provisionally, hesitantly, with many reservations, we may divide works in open form into three classes according to the motive of the artist: to express a philosophy, to gain a perspective, or to fulfill the requirements of a style. (Perhaps this triad includes a good many of the motives for literary creation in any form.) Needless to say, these categories are not mutually exclusive; nor, for that matter, are they wholly inclusive. Burlesque is a particular patron of the form unexpectedly opened on itself: "Don't worry," says Peer Gynt, as he is supposed to be drowning, "the hero never dies till the fifth act." There is, perhaps, another sort of openness which derives from mixture of genres—opera libretti, for example, or so-called "shaped verses," as a category, or some sorts of parody. But the three main categories seem to me to account for a good many of the most striking examples of the open form in literature. In each case they involve and may be thought of as expressing incongruity or disparity, either in the thing seen or in the mind seeing it or in the mode of literary vision.

Most aesthetic theories seem to suppose that a work of art which is not ultimately unified thematically, ideologically, emotionally, imagistically, and on the narrative level —or which does not at least do its best to be unified in some or all of these ways—must remain diffuse and undirected. Conflicts must be resolved; knots of one sort must be untied so that those of another sort can be retied; varying themes are drawn together so that a mere "end" can be elevated to the dignity of a "conclusion." Some sort of unity is thus to be imposed by the artist on his material or drawn out of it; if it is not, the work is not a unified whole and so may be thought to lack not only a beginning, a middle, and an end but all structural proportion, which can only be measured against a finite, and so closed, framework. This is logic which a poem by Donne or Crashaw, a novel by Cervantes, or a play by Brecht seems flagrantly to defy. There is no beginning or end to "The Weeper"; it is a string of stanzas on a theme, which goes on for a while and then stops. The pearls could be strung in another order, and in greater or lesser number, without the slightest harm to the poem. The episodes of *Don Quixote* are not organic to the structure of the novel; there could be more or less of them; some are burlesque, some are serious, and some are just plain puzzling. There is a main point to the novel, but it is made with no sense of economy at all and is often blurred and overlaid by miscellaneous materials. Where in such a work does the mind find any resting place or resolution? And how can one pass aesthetic judgment on works like *A Doll's House* or *The Good Woman of Setzuan* when all the time they are nipping at one's ankles and declaring with unmuzzled ferocity that they are not mere stage plays and one is not a mere aesthetic spectator—that one must take part in the action as a moral judge and see through the shabby delusions of stage appearance and aesthetic self-sufficiency?

A characteristic, then, of one sort of open-formed work is the direct and unmediated quality of its relation to the audience. By imputing to its reader no character at all, or a condition purely negative, the work in closed form disguises or minimizes its essentially relativist relation to the reader. Works in the open form make this relativism explicit. They often imply an image of man as an essentially divided and self-antagonistic creature. Although he may be ignorant of this fact at first, the work brings him to a realization of it; and to do so it must stand at once closer to the reader and further from its own actions or characters. Its proper effect always precludes simple identification between reader and character; an element of self-consciousness enters into the proper reaction to the work in open form. The forging of this self-conscious reaction has, indeed, sometimes led to diffuseness and a kind of episodic, discursive treatment of themes. On the other hand, it is a complex effect in itself, involving a balance of contradictory elements; and the work which produces it is bound to be specially, and complexly, structured.

Of course when one undertakes to make a man conscious of himself, it helps to have some notion of what his self actually is; simply on prudential terms, one is probably unwise to write on the assumption that man will have any particular, pronounced character. The more special and peculiar the commitment, the more perishable it is likely to be. But this is mere worldly wisdom; from another aspect, the odd and individual point of view is the only one worth exploring. Indeed, without putting a premium on novelty or magnitude as such, one may attribute value to any work of art which helps man to see experience from a new point of view or to see further into it than an old point of view has allowed him. This is no negation of formalism, but a supplement to it. Structure and invention, like those older terms "judgment" and "wit," may be correlative values; the dichotomy is as old as Aristotle, who tells us that a living organism or a work of art must have not only an orderly arrangement of parts but a certain magnitude. And in the balancing of these qualities there is ample scope for all the subtleties of formalist analysis without that impulsion to Procrustean ruthlessness which seems to accompany critical monism of all sorts. A formalist aesthetic, which accounts for the effect of a work of art in terms of its internal organization, certainly has much to contribute. Pedagogically, indeed, it is incomparably useful; in terms of critical definitions it is susceptible of an elegant sharpness and clarity. But when exclusively and categorically held, there is a danger of its degenerating into an aesthetic mechanics. And I know of no compelling reason why it should preclude the recognition of other literary values: among others, the opening and exploitation of new subject matter, the projection of an intense state of mind, or the inconclusive pursuit of two contradictory ideas irrespective of whether they are reconciled into a formal unity.

Indeed, literature, even in its most primitive forms, seems to stand in two relations to experience. Stories are told because they summarize and clarify the common experience of the race. They are exemplary and moralistic; by means of them the multitudinous details of life can be codified and organized. For such productions, arrangement is of the essence; quite aside from the fact that they are socially oriented, and so disposed to make use of mnemonic, repetitive, and controlling rhythmic devices, their purpose from the beginning is to manage material which is already common in itself, to give it a structure and a meaning. Such productions respond very conveniently to Kenneth Burke's fourfold division of function; they may serve as prayer, chart, game, or dream—and, for that matter, as lesson or warning. Whatever the level of generalization and symbolization, they are an acting out of a situation and an organization of the emotional responses appropriate to it. To such works the closed form is clearly appropriate; indeed, it is almost mandatory.

On the other hand, stories are often told not because they summarize the everyday but because they report on the unfamiliar—because they extend experience instead of compacting it. The romance is a form almost as old as the epic but psychologically opposed to it; various, episodic, and extended, where the epic centers on a single hero and a single typical action, it is bounded only by the invention of the author and the physical endurance of the audience. (Popular Italian romances, one recalls, were quite literally endless; the audience circulated continually, but the story-teller had a lifetime ahead of him and an interminable stock of anecdotes to play with.) Yet the relation between these two forms is not truly antithetical but complementary; epic codifies and imposes values on a world which romance explores and enlarges.

This is not an argument that romances or any other work must necessarily be written in the open form but an asser-tion of an interest and a value which literature has for us, other than its structuring of experience or of itself. We like to see a problem "worked out to the end," a familiar premise followed rigorously to its final conclusion; we like also to see ground broken for new premises and new conclusions, even though the author may not know what all these conclusions are or how to reconcile them with one another. On both scores, the literary work in open form may claim a special interest. The discovery of impasse is often a singular experience around which a work that is closed in all other respects may be structured; it may also be caused to reflect interestingly on the qualities of vision and character which are responsible for the impasse. In addition, the consequences of impasse may be traced out in opposing directions to two separate finalities or to several or to none at all. The measure of such a work is not its structural unity but its total relevance and intensity. One cannot, of course, show that relevance and intensity are "there" in a work of art, as it can be shown that verbal

irony or double meanings or structural patterns are "there."
Relevance and intensity exist only in relation to a particular
reader, who may or may not be susceptible to their impact.
But then, however many formal qualities one discovers in
the work of art, one is always left with a gap between the
qualities themselves and the effect they are supposed to
produce on a particular reader. Silence on this point is
safe but it is not very golden.

Dim as they are in any abstract sense, relevance and intensity have a certain clear historical significance. Herrick
was clearly irrelevant to the circumstances of 1649, and
Donne was as thoroughly irrelevant to Tennyson as Tennyson was to Dylan Thomas. Professional littérateurs sometimes feel bound to pretend that all works of art are relevant
to them, and there is no denying that sympathy and flexi-
bility of temper will accomplish a good deal. Yet there is,
in the end, a pretense about universal adaptability. Pope
is no worse a poet now than he was in the eighteenth century, but he speaks to a smaller area of our awareness—he
is less relevant. Hopkins seemed totally irrelevant to his
own day; we have seen him burgeon into the status of a
major author and may perhaps live to see his decline. Relevance is something more than fashion, though vogues are
often an expression of it, as well as of other things; neither
is relevance merely to be measured quantitatively, as intellectual agreement on X number of points. Relevance is
nothing less than an author's congruity with the patterns
of thought and feeling diffused through an age, his gift for
settling upon those issues which an age will count crucially
important. As such, it is a distinct criterion external to the
work proper; and, though not easily measured or pre-
dicted, it must be reckoned with.

Intensity is another criterion the need for which is rendered particularly apparent by works in open form. But is this not a familiar acquaintance of the formalist critic, an old friend who has, at various times, passed under the various names of "tension," "texture," or "ambiguity"? The distinctions are, admittedly, not clean-cut; but "intensity," simply because it is so untechnical a term, seems useful to describe a quality of emotional response which may or may not be associated with the technical qualities denoted by the other words. Thomas' "Religious Sonnets" give an intense imaginative experience by means of various devices of witty opposition, ambiguity, and so on; but the thirtieth stanza of Keats' "Eve of St. Agnes" and the last stanza of Herbert's "Love" also give an intense experience without using any such devices. Not only perfect simplicity but unresolved duplicity may be associated with intense imaginative experiences; in fact, intense literary effects may be achieved in many ways: by thoughts and language novel, beautiful, or harmonious in themselves, by sheer mass and weight of materials (as in documentary and social novels and the poetry of Whitman), or by the blending of materials, manners, and emotional overtones in such wry and unresolved ways as this book has been concerned to explore.

Among all these varieties and gradations of intensity I can see no grounds for discrimination between the categorically superior and inferior. Any reader or author who chooses may declare any of these effects beyond a pale of his own devising; on some such grounds as these, recently, Keats has been declared no poet, Milton dismissed as idiotic, and Tolstoi simply written off as of no literary account. But the formulator of a proper theory of literary values ought, I think, to base his declarations on all literary experience, even though ultimately he will distinguish higher and lower forms of it; and perhaps, when one stands at the beginning of such an enterprise, the more one is aware of oddities and incongruities, the better.

Admittedly there is a place where the effort at intensity fails through lack of verbal craft, through the use of too much artifice, through monotony or thinness or clumsiness or some other clear deficiency. There are places, too, where the pursuit of intensity for its own sake verges on the factitious. And everyone is familiar with those intense and vivid literary experiences which one outgrows, mansions, which, with the passage of time, come to seem hovels —the experience of Shelley in time of puberty. But a criterion which measures everything easily is probably measuring nothing important. It is harder to talk about intensity and relevance than about witty ambiguities; but it is harder to talk about witty ambiguities than about the use of capital letters in *Paradise Lost*, the sexual proclivities of Samuel Butler, or the wrestling hold used by Beowulf upon Grendel. One's only excuse for selecting the more difficult topic is the hope of saying something adequate about the effects which literature has and the ways in which it achieves them.

These issues are all rendered particularly acute and troubling by those works of open form which deliberately elect to produce an impure and troublesome literary effect. "I come to disquiet" says an author like Gide. And he is right; he disquiets us and makes us uncertain even about the standards by which we might proclaim him a great disquieter. And yet, why else does the continuing effort of criticism, comparison, and judgment go on, if not to enable us to absorb and control even the great disquieter, the most mercurial and destructive of writers?

A vessel for transport of the universal solvent—the metaphor parodies a current ambition of critics and criticism. Yet in the end something comes of it all—the mind widens to admit what it first rejected, the new hypothesis is seen as a negation but also as an enlargement of the old. We learn from the formalist criticism and also from a denial of it; and though the work of art is never made and can never be made the same for all those who experience it, the range of variation may be defined, the conditions of judgment clarified, the consequences of various assumptions worked out. One greatness of the great disquieter lies in the great truths for which he clears the ground; one greatness of the great truths is the great disquieting questions which are cracked out of them. To see things in this way explains nothing; but it may give us patience to accept much of the structure of our present insights and audacity to venture against all closed and tightly organized critical systems, as the artists, without ever bothering their heads about it, have been venturing for a long, long time.

Index